The Young Activist's Guide to
BUILDING A GREEN MOVEMENT
+ CHANGING THE WORLD

The Young Activist's Guide to

BUILDING A GREEN MOVEMENT + CHANGING THE WORLD

WITHDRAWN

Sharon J. Smith

TEN SPEED PRESS
Berkeley

To all the **BOLD AND VISIONARY YOUNG LEADERS** at the heart of the movement for sustainability—**YOU ARE AN INSPIRATION**.

Copyright © 2011 by the Earth Island Institute, Inc.
Foreword copyright © 2011 by julia butterfly hill

All rights reserved.
Published in the United States by Ten Speed Press, an imprint of the Crown Publishing Group, a division of Random House, Inc., New York.
www.crownpublishing.com
www.tenspeed.com

Ten Speed Press and the Ten Speed Press colophon are registered trademarks of Random House, Inc.

Library of Congress Cataloging-in-Publication Data
Smith, Sharon J.
  The young activist's guide to building a green movement + changing the world / Sharon J. Smith.
     p. cm.
  Includes index.
  Summary: "A practical, step-by-step guide for young activists to planning and executing successful environmental campaigns, featuring strategies and lessons learned from Earth Island Institute's Brower Youth Award winners"—Provided by publisher.
  1. Environmentalism. 2. Green movement. 3. Youth—Conduct of life.
  I. Title.
  GE195.S555 2011
  333.72—dc22
                    2010043750

ISBN 978-1-58008-561-8

Printed in the United States of America using vegetable-based inks on 100 percent chlorine-free, post-consumer fiber manufactured using biogas energy. The use of this recycled paper has saved 38 trees, nearly 23,000 gallons of water, more than 5,000 pounds of air emissions, and almost 2,500 pounds of solid waste.

Design by Katy Brown

10 9 8 7 6 5 4 3 2 1

First Edition

CONTENTS

FOREWORD

You have opened a book that has the power to support you in changing your life and changing your world. Yes, that's right, it's *your* world. And it's *our* world, and it's about time we take it personally! You are taking the first step by reading this guide. But we all know it's one thing to feel that call stirring deep within us, and it's another thing all together to confront our fears.

I climbed up into Luna in a Northern California redwood forest on December 10, 1997. I touched ground again for the first time on December 18, 1999, holding an agreement with the logging company to permanently protect Luna and a buffer area around the tree. Mine is the longest tree-sit in our collective story. I am not telling you this so you'll be impressed by me, but because I know beyond a shadow of a doubt that we all have our own "tree."

Your tree is whatever issue in life is calling you to be bigger and bolder than you ever could have imagined. The call is so powerful that you don't have the choice to be silent and walk away. Because you know in your heart that the time is now for you—yes, *you*—to step up, step out, and be a force for the world you envision living and *thriving* in.

When I first considered getting involved in the campaign to protect the ancient redwoods, I had all kinds of "not enough" conversations with myself. "What can I do? I don't know how to be an 'activist.' I'm not even sure I know what that means! I don't have any experience. There are plenty of people working on this issue, they don't need me." These thoughts and more were running amuck in my mind, trying to keep me from taking a risk and just going for it. Most everyone involved in and committed to making a real difference in the world has felt these same fears and concerns.

But when I was chatting with the universe, trying to figure out if I should get involved or not, the answer that came to me was, "Julia, if you know something is wrong, if you know that an injustice is happening and you have the opportunity to say or do something and you don't, your *inactions* are as much a part of that injustice as the actions of others." That answer came to me again and again, so loud and so clear that I knew it was time to act—even though I had absolutely no clue how or what I was going to do.

Never let the fact that you don't know how to do something stop you from doing it anyway. We don't always know how we are going to get from point A to point B. Sometimes we aren't even sure where or what the points are, let alone how to navigate them. But I can tell you from experience that as soon as we get ourselves in motion, the path becomes clear. The people we need to meet show up, and the necessary tools and resources become apparent as well. After all, you found this book, right?

Now more than ever in our collective story, we need as many of us as possible to stand up and be courageous in our vision. Each one of us is a unique gift and each role we play is equal in importance. What is challenging for me is a walk in the park for someone else and vice versa. It is up to you to step into your greatest self—who you are is who you are meant to be and your contribution is vital.

Remember to enjoy the journey and to celebrate the victory that happens every single time you choose to care. And from the very depths of my heart, thank you for having the courage to put that care into action, to live your life as a legacy today and for future generations. May this book help you make the difference you are committed to making and become the very best *you* that you can possibly be.

In loving service and deep gratitude,
julia butterfly hill

ACKNOWLEDGMENTS

Without the vision, support, and best thinking of two individuals, this book would not be in your hands. I want to shower abundant thanks and praise on my colleague Jason Dove Mark for his thoughtful edits, helping bring clarity and life to my ideas. He was my copilot on this project, start to finish. Katherine Cowles of Cowles-Ryan Literary Agency saw the potential of this book to be a useful tool for young activists and helped birth the idea. Jason and Kitty, I'm tremendously grateful for all of your contributions.

Thanks to Julie Bennett, my remarkably talented and committed editor at Ten Speed Press; your coaching helped me embrace the writing process and produce my best work.

The Earth Island Institute and Brower Youth Awards community consists of some of the most dedicated change-makers on the planet. Thank you John Knox, David Phillips, Kevin Connelly, Ellen Manchester, and Anisha Desai for your moral support and constant backing. Our extended community of supporters has made the Brower Youth Awards so dynamic: thank you Eric Kessler, Marika Holmgren, Jennifer Snyder, Thao Pham, Nadine Weil, Michael Mitrani, Adrienne Maree Brown, Kyle MacDonald, Andre Carothers, Adam Werbach, Lynn Hirshfield, and so many others. Brower Youth Award recipients: I am blessed and humbled to know and work with you. And the Brower family members—Barbara, Ken, Shirley, Joe, John, Rosemary, Kathryn, and David—are incredible individuals who have kept Dave Brower's legacy alive.

I would like to acknowledge all of the mentors and guides who have helped me on my journey as an organizer, activist, and now author, but listing you all would fill many pages of this book. You know who you are, and I have been shaped by your influence.

Finally, a thank-you to my family: Mom, Dad, and Steve. You are my backbone, and I am ever grateful.

CONTRIBUTORS

My helpful team of readers included Brower Youth Award recipients Dave Karpf, Ariana Katovich, Andrew Hunt, Jon Warnow, Timothy DenHerder-Thomas, Jessian Choy, Marisol Becerra, Elissa Smith, Zander Srodes, Ruben Vogt, Sierra Crane-Murdoch, Jessica Assaf, Alexander Lin, Amir Nadav, Whitney Cushing, Rachel Barge, Lily Dong, May Boeve, and Ethan Schaffer, as well as my Earth Island Institute colleagues Anisha Desai and Jason Dove Mark. Additional readers included Megan Dunn, Luke Janes, Helena Janes, Matthew Carroll, and Deborah Moore.

Chapter 2, Create an Action Plan, and chapter 4, Spread Your Message, drew heavily on the writing and contributions of Brenna Holzhauer, education manager, and Sean S. Miller, education director, who oversee Earth Day Network's Education Department. Brenna and Sean continue this effort—which grew out of the first Earth Day, a national teach-in for the environment—into the twenty-first-century learning environment. They manage Earth Day Network's global network of more than twenty-five thousand educators and related programs promoting environmental education, green schools, and campus sustainability. Find out more at www.earthday.org.

Richard Graves was a significant contributor to chapter 8, Make Media Headlines, as was Rachel Barge to chapter 9, Grow the Green.

INTRODUCTION
IF YOU WANT TO GO FAR, GO TOGETHER

A movement is brewing. The fact that you're here reading this book is no accident. We are on the verge of some of the most significant societal changes in human history. We have to be. We can't continue on our current path any longer.

Our planet's systems are on the brink. We're in the middle of the sixth major global extinction crisis, with more than seventeen thousand species at risk due to human activity—including animals like the polar bear, the hippopotamus, and one-third of all shark and fish species. The current extinction rate is more than a thousand times higher than the natural rate. The Himalayan glaciers, which provide drinking water to well over a billion people, are rapidly melting, and the global sea level is expected to rise between 0.6 and 2 feet by the beginning of the next century due to climate change.

It's amazing that you and I were born at this incredible moment in time. Modern humans have two hundred thousand years of history on this planet, and each generation has increased the richness of promise for the next. We were born into a world of possibilities—for work, love, travel, education, health, and personal fulfillment—greater than at any other moment in human history. But it's possible that we're at the top of a roller-coaster ride: that although every generation before us has worked to make more opportunities available for their children, our generation will live in the moment when possibilities decline because our earth's natural systems are becoming damaged beyond repair.

1

You probably hear a lot about how to make personal lifestyle choices to live more sustainably: ride your bike, use public transportation, recycle, switch out your lightbulbs for compact fluorescents, and buy organic and local foods, for starters. Making personal lifestyle shifts is important not only for the actual benefits to the planet, but also because we need to model the values we're espousing! However, even if we get every single one of our friends, family members, and neighbors to make these personal changes, it won't be enough. This book is about engaging in the larger battles that are going to transform our society—working for institutional, business, and political solutions to the environmental crises confronting us.

An African proverb says, "If you want to go fast, go alone. If you want to go far, go together." To build movements capable of addressing the most challenging environmental problems we face today, we have to work together. Of course, any of us working solo is capable of making a difference in our homes and communities. But many issues—like global warming, rainforest destruction, and air and water pollution—are just too big to be solved by individuals working in isolation.

That's why we organize—to make sure that we're not acting alone but working together as one. On the cusp of the greatest challenge our generation has ever seen, it's imperative that we as young people use our power, passion, and voices to build a green movement and create a sustainable future.

THE BROWER YOUTH AWARDS

While we hear lots about the adults who are solving environmental problems, an enormous amount of groundbreaking work has been led by youth—ordinary individuals like you who simply saw a problem and then organized others to take action to make a difference.

Throughout this book I will spotlight success stories from youth like Jessie-Ruth Corkins, who saved her school $90,000 by greening its heating system for a science project, and Billy Parish, whose small student group became one of the most influential coalitions in America addressing climate change. These eco-heroes have made headlines for passing legislation, founding lasting nonprofits, protecting local wildlands from bulldozers and chainsaws, and raising millions of dollars for sustainability—all before their

BROWER YOUTH AWARDS

You will hear about dozens of young green leaders throughout this book; for more inspiration, look at the Brower Youth Awards site (www.broweryouthawards.org), where you can read stories and watch films about each of the Brower Youth Award recipients since 2000, plus find out about exciting opportunities in the green movement.

twenty-third birthdays! To recognize this incredible work, these champions of the planet were awarded Earth Island Institute's Brower Youth Award (BYA), North America's top prize for young environmental leaders. Some had previous campaign experience; others were complete novices, starting from scratch.

David Brower, the namesake of the awards, was one of the twentieth century's most influential environmental leaders. A famous mountain climber in the 1930s, he went on to become the first executive director of the Sierra Club and led conservation campaigns for more than sixty years. Among his many accomplishments, Brower worked to establish nine new national parks and seashores, including Cape Cod, North Cascades, and the Redwoods, and helped gain passage of the Wilderness Act of 1964 to protect millions of acres of public land. In 1982, Brower founded Earth Island Institute, an organization that fosters and supports dozens of innovative environmental projects around the world. Above all, Brower believed in the power of youth to be real leaders in the sustainability movement.

FROM PASSION TO ACTION

If you are just getting started in tackling the root causes of environmental destruction, this book can be your partner and your guide. Let's say you've already decided to stop drinking bottled water but want to do more—such as transition your entire campus away from bottled water. I will show you how to design a campaign to make it happen. If you want to do more than simply buy organic, local foods for your own consumption, the Brower Youth Award winners will model how to launch a campus or community garden to encourage more people to make the same decision. And if you've already replaced your incandescent lightbulbs at home with compact fluorescents, this book will point you to strategies and tools for doing an energy audit and designing an energy-saving plan for your entire campus or a local business.

Individual actions feel good, but only collective actions lead to lasting solutions. There are many ways to take your activism beyond a recycling program or a beach cleanup, and that's what this book is all about. Chapters 1–3 will help you find your calling, join or build a team of like-minded people to organize around your cause, and develop an action plan. Chapters 4–7 detail ways to grow a community of supporters through educational activities, plan protests, lobby and influence public policy, and run campaigns to change corporate practices. Chapters 8 and 9 will help you attract resources and attention to support your cause, as an individual and in the context of a group. Chapter 10 is designed to help you improve your campus's environmental footprint. If you're not a student, check out this chapter for tips on working with decision makers, advertising your work, and adapting campus greening models for your city or region. The final chapter details a personal action plan for taking your activism to the next level.

There's no need to read the book straight through—you can go right to the chapter that most interests you, or pick and choose from the offerings at hand. At the end of each chapter, you'll find websites, groups, and other resources listed that focus on that area of activism.

I'd like to end this introduction with the words of Anna Rose, the founder of the Australian Youth Climate Coalition: "I know we're running out of time, and that the best time to be doing this work, this transition to a sustainable economy and society, was twenty years ago. But you know the second best time to do it? It's today."

Now, let's get started!

01

FIND YOUR PASSION

HOW TO JOIN THE ENVIRONMENTAL MOVEMENT

Have you ever heard the expression, "Don't let the perfect be the enemy of the good"? When I was beginning my activist journey in college, I spent years trying to decide what issue to work on because I wanted my efforts to be perfectly matched to my interests. I felt like I never had either enough background information to choose just one issue or enough time to devote to all of my passions. If I worked on rainforest conservation in the Amazon, who would work on shutting down toxic waste dumps in the United States? If I worked to save the community garden from closure, how would I find the time to protest the oil company polluting my hometown coastline?

As I waited for the perfect opportunity to get involved, my college career drew to a close—and I hadn't gotten involved in any issue at all! Over time, I realized that there is no "most critical" or "most important" issue; instead, we all need to work for our biggest passion. My passion is forest protection. As a child, I pored over books and stories about temperate and tropical rainforests. In high school, I decided I would one day study abroad in Costa Rica. When I was nineteen I headed there to study ecology, and I followed that up with a research stint in Panama at the Smithsonian's tropical research station, where I was able to connect with some of the world's top tropical ecologists. After my college graduation, I dove into an effort to protect old-growth forests in the United States, and I've never regretted my first campaign choice.

While we face an intimidating number of environmental challenges, here's the good news: millions of individuals worldwide are getting involved. You don't have to fix everything yourself. Are you outraged by the inhumane conditions of factory farms? Does it break your heart to hear about mountaintop coal mining in Appalachia, modern-day slavery in polluting gold mines, or the climate crisis leading to drought, wildfires, destructive weather, and species extinction around the world? Figure out what your gut and your heart are most excited about, and work on that issue. Activism can be difficult and slow going, but if you truly care about the issue, you'll be far more likely to stick with it when the going gets rough, rather than burn out and drop out.

Most people become activists because they are compelled to protect the places and people they love. And in many cases, young people become activists because an issue finds them—not the other way around. Ethan Schaffer, for example, got involved in the sustainable foods movement after looking for answers to the question of why he and other young kids were suffering from serious illnesses like cancer.

SUCCESS STORY
GET YOUR HANDS DIRTY When **Ethan Schaffer** was fifteen,
he was diagnosed with lymphoma cancer. He left his friends in ninth grade and underwent five months of intensive and brutal chemotherapy. Fortunately, the treatment worked and he survived. But the experience changed him. He began to question why kids were getting cancer and started asking what he could do to create change. Eventually this led Ethan to explore healthy and sustainable living by working on organic farms in New Zealand. Revitalized by the experience, Ethan realized that the solution to both health and environmental problems lay in individuals learning to live sustainably. When he returned to the United States in 2001, he launched

GrowFood.org. Grow Food helps people experience sustainable living by connecting them with opportunities to work on organic farms. Less than a decade later, the program has connected more than twenty thousand people with opportunities to live, eat, and grow food more sustainably on nearly two thousand farms in all fifty states and in forty-one countries.

"We need to **GET TOXIC CHEMICALS OFF THE FARM AND OUT OF THE FOOD SYSTEM.** Organic farming is good for both the planet and people."

—ETHAN SCHAFFER

Like Ethan, you might choose to work on an issue because it affects your health or the health of friends or family members. Do you or your family members have asthma because local industries are polluting the air? Do you surf in an area with contaminated water? Many of the most passionate advocates I have met are driven by a personal experience dealing with asthma, sickness, cancer, or the unnecessary death of a loved one due to an illness caused by contamination.

Think about your community—your neighborhood, town, or city. Could you work to protect and establish more parks and green space as Connie Shahid did?

SUCCESS STORY
FINDING YOUR PASSION WHEN YOU'RE NOT LOOKING
Seventeen-year-old **Connie Shahid** wasn't always familiar with environmental issues. A senior in high school, she lived in a San Francisco neighborhood called Bayview-Hunters Point, a polluted and economically depressed area surrounded by freeways, a power plant, and a naval shipyard. She was looking for a job when she encountered Literacy for Environmental Justice (LEJ), an organization that addressed the health and environmental concerns in her community. She began working to combat the destructive effects of industrialization and landfills on the native wetlands that in turn improved the air and water quality. Connie engaged

other young people in the effort by putting up posters, speaking to youth groups, and doing outreach in her neighborhood. She served as a model and a mentor to the younger participants as they repaired a community garden, built a 1,200-square-foot shade house to host native plant seedlings, and created a strong community of youth activists who cared about community stewardship.

"Before working with LEJ, I didn't even know what environmental justice was. **IT'S CHANGED ME,** because now **I'M MORE CONSCIOUS.**"

—CONNIE SHAHID

© Karen Smith

Connie wasn't looking for a way to get involved in the environmental movement when she ended up finding her passion. If you're wondering what issue is right for you, start close to home, as she did. What can you do to lessen your city's environmental footprint, add green space, or clean up the air and water? If you're a student, starting on campus is a good bet. What are the major opportunities for getting involved at your school? Do you lack a recycling program? Do you want to introduce environmental science courses to the curriculum or launch a campus organic garden?

One strategy for turning passion into action is to identify a meaningful environmental change you have made in your personal life and figure out how to bring that change to a larger group of people or an entire institution, like a campus, your town, or a business. You start by making changes in your personal life, like eating organic food. Organizing takes this one step further by looking at how you can institutionalize those changes to benefit more people (say, starting an organic garden open to community members or convincing your campus to buy at least 20 percent of its produce from organic farmers). The first is personal change; the second is real change for society. Of course, organizing is more work, but its impacts are much more influential, as Diana Lopez can attest!

SUCCESS STORY
ROOTS OF CHANGE Diana Lopez, twenty, recognized the challenges faced by her community in the east side of San Antonio, Texas, due to the lack of large grocery stores and places to get fresh, organic, or local produce. A growing number of people in her family and community had cancer or diabetes, and she began to look at the linkage between food and health. Talking with elders in her community, she learned that the farming techniques of a hundred years ago kept the ground healthy and the food safe—many of the same techniques now used in organic gardening. Diana decided to start growing her own organic food—and to offer the option for healthy eating to her community. She cofounded the Roots of Change garden to serve as an educational center and positive space for community gathering. Since 2007 she has worked with hundreds of youth and adults to create a native plant and food garden and to host educational sessions, coordinate student workdays, and provide locally grown produce for the community.

"EVERYONE DESERVES the right to **A CLEAN, HEALTHY ENVIRONMENT,** regardless of your color or economic status." **—DIANA LOPEZ**

© Han Shan

Or maybe you're like Dave Karpf. He knew he wanted to get more deeply involved in the environmental movement but wasn't sure where to start. Not driven by any particular issue, he looked to experienced organizers to find a way to plug in.

SUCCESS STORY
SAVE THE BELT WOODS Dave Karpf's experience with environmental activism started when he was a junior in high school. As the head of his environmental club, he wanted to find something to work on beyond monthly roadside cleanups. So Dave reached out to the local chapter of the Sierra Club and asked what they were working on. From them, he

learned about the Coalition to Save the Belt Woods, an effort to protect the last old-growth forest in Maryland. He had never been to the Belt Woods, but he and his friends cared about wilderness, and this was an opportunity to make a real difference.

Dave created a new group, Montgomery County Student Environmental Activists (MCSEA), which united environmentally minded high school students at a half-dozen schools in his area. Within three months, MCSEA had gathered over one thousand petition signatures urging the state legislature to protect the forest. The group then hand-delivered the petitions to state delegates, lobbied them on the issue, and helped organize a rally in the state capital. The coalition had been working on the issue for five years, and MCSEA proved instrumental in finally saving the forest. Legislators were surprised to see high school students so enthusiastic about the issue, and that made a real difference in the final decision.

"It was only because we **CONNECTED OURSELVES TO THE LARGER ENVIRONMENTAL COMMUNITY** and asked 'how can we help?' that we were able to achieve victory." **—DAVE KARPF**

Dave took his experience with MCSEA and went on to direct the Sierra Student Coalition, training hundreds of other students to run campaigns on a variety of issues. Like Dave, you can start your environmental activism by locating a community of like-minded individuals already working on environmental issues on your campus, online, or in your community. Find out what these groups are working on, then figure out how you can help them build their power. Later, after you've built relationships with these group members and achieved victory on the hot issues, suggest that they tackle your passion as their next project. Organizing is a community activity, and we're almost never starting from scratch.

If you haven't yet decided which issue you want to work for, there's absolutely nothing wrong with being involved in many issues. In fact, that can be a great way to get educated about a range of causes and get a taste for many different forms of activism. If you're just getting started, I highly recommend exploring everything and anything that calls out to you. That's what citizen activism is all about: expressing your values and your beliefs.

However, many young activists spread themselves too thin. The more issues you work on, the less likely you are to make a meaningful difference in any one arena. The most successful individuals and groups tend to focus on one or two main issues and relentlessly campaign until they win. Once you've found an issue that you're really passionate about, try to use the 80-20 rule (an idea that we activists have adopted from the business world): spend 80 percent of your time, energy, and resources working on that issue, and use the remaining 20 percent to explore other issues that you feel passionate about.

If you're still looking for your cause, here are a handful of the most pressing environmental challenges of the twenty-first century and related topics within each area:

> Climate change and energy production (global warming, energy conservation, renewable energy production, fossil fuel use, nuclear energy and waste, mountaintop coal mining)

> Waste creation (electronic waste, landfills, recycling, composting, incineration)

> Toxins and pollution (air and water pollution, acid rain, oil spills, smog, pesticides and herbicides, carcinogens, heavy metals)

> Land and species conservation (restoration of degraded ecosystems, species extinction, public lands preservation and access, wilderness areas, deforestation, illegal logging and poaching)

> Urban planning (sprawl, urban renewal, green building, population growth)

> Agriculture and food (organic and local foods, urban gardens, monoculture farming, meat production, grazing, desertification, soil conservation, genetically modified foods)

> Water resources (dams, drinking water, privatization of water resources)

> Ocean conservation (overfishing, shark finning, whaling, ocean dumping, ocean acidification)

> ➤ Animal rights (factory farms, animals as food and clothing, hunting and trapping)

> ➤ Public education (consumerism, environmental education)

Groups like the Sierra Club (www.sierraclub.org), Greenpeace (www.greenpeace.org), and Friends of the Earth (www.foe.org) offer information about a number of the topics just listed. Read background information, watch videos, and research case studies of areas under threat and pressing issues until you find one that calls out to you.

Probably the best way to get a read on the environmental movement is to check out the major youth networks. The groups listed at the end of this chapter are all uniting to create change on a series of campaigns. If you're not ready to design your own campaign or launch your own group, or you like the idea of working on large-scale environmental campaigns (too big for a local group to do alone), team up with one of these existing youth networks to make change collectively.

GET EDUCATED

Once you have found your cause, it's time to get educated.

Research is critical; you need to get rooted in your issue before launching full-steam ahead into action. It's one thing to go out and "do good," but by whose standards are you doing good and to what end? While there is always more to learn about an issue, and you don't want to get stuck in the research stage, spend some time learning about the issue to provide a solid foundation for your future organizing. With a little bit of research, you'll be better prepared to launch a strategic and useful action plan, without stepping on anybody's toes. You don't want to burst onto the scene without realizing there's another local group in town that's been working on your issue for five years (and knows what has worked, and what hasn't, over that time).

To find out more about your issue of choice, watch documentary films, read newspaper articles and excerpts from books, and do extensive internet research. Ask your friends and family what they know about the topic. If you are working on a local issue, start having conversations with the people who are directly affected. You can do formal surveys or simply start up friendly conversations to learn from the people who know the subject most intimately. Who else is working on this issue on your campus, in your community, and beyond? Find out how those groups are addressing the matter. Then you can decide to either join up with existing efforts or launch your own new group to tackle the issue.

If you can't find a local organization that is doing the kind of work you are interested in, your best bet might be to start your own group. Before starting a new group, however, make sure you actually need one. Start by finding out the history of environmental organizations on your campus or in your community. Have previous groups gone dormant? If so, why? What teachers or civic leaders have supported environmental and progressive projects? What organizations currently do progressive work on campus or in your town? Who are the key leaders in those groups? Are there community groups tackling your issue that would welcome a youth presence?

If you find a group with a similar mission, consider joining—perhaps you can create a new subcommittee or project group to work on your issue. Launching a group from scratch can be a lot of work, and there's no need to reinvent the wheel if another group has made some headway. However, if a similar group doesn't exist, or you're not drawn to the people or issues covered by existing groups, then it could be time to launch your own.

NEXT STOP: CREATE AN ACTION PLAN

Whether you launch a new group or join an existing one, one of the most valuable skills you can bring to the table is strategic planning. In the next chapter, I'll show you how to develop a thoughtful and achievable action plan.

RESOURCES

Energy Action Coalition, www.energyactioncoalition.org Launched in part by a former Brower Youth Award recipient and with numerous past recipients in leadership roles, the Energy Action Coalition is easily one of the most powerful student networks in North America. With fifty partner organizations, the coalition unites young people to fight for and win clean energy and climate policies on their campuses, while demanding that governments and corporations do the same.

Roots & Shoots, www.rootsandshoots.org Roots & Shoots, founded by renowned primatologist Dr. Jane Goodall, works with tens of thousands of young people in nearly one hundred countries to implement successful community service projects and global campaigns. Roots & Shoots focuses on wildlife, as well as the environment and people-centered programming.

Sierra Student Coalition (SSC), www.ssc.org SSC is the student-run arm of the Sierra Club and has produced more than ten Brower Youth Award winners. With a presence on over 250 campuses across the country, SSC provides great support, training, and resources, including fellowships for college and university students. Earth Island Institute founder David Brower was the primary architect of the Sierra Club's lobbying and political efforts as the club's first executive director from 1952–69.

Sierra Youth Coalition, www.syc-cjs.org The Sierra Youth Coalition is SSC's counterpart in Canada, operating in eighty colleges and universities and fifty high schools.

Student Environmental Action Coalition (SEAC), www.seac.org SEAC, a loose and nonhierarchical student-run national network of students and campus environmental groups (mostly college, some high schools), champions environmental justice campaigns at the local and national level.

Student Public Interest Research Groups (PIRGs), www.student pirgs.org For more than forty years, the PIRGs have been working on environmental protection and consumer advocacy at university campuses across the United States. They offer students the skills and opportunity to investigate big social problems, come up with practical solutions, convince the media and public to pay attention, and get decision makers to act.

02
CREATE AN ACTION PLAN

SET YOUR GOALS AND CHOOSE YOUR TACTICS

So now you've got an issue to address and some basic ideas of ways you might be able to make a difference. If you're entering an existing group, they've probably got a clear plan for how to achieve victory on their issues. However, if you're starting a group from scratch, it's time to focus on building your team and then creating an action plan (also called a "campaign plan" in social-change circles). I recommend starting an organization that initially rallies around a specific goal, such as bringing solar power to your campus or shutting down a local toxic waste incinerator, rather than bringing together a group to address climate change or environmental injustice more generally. I have seen far too many groups spinning their wheels for months on end as dozens of people chime in on potential directions.

Groups tend to be more effective when they are rallied around a specific common goal. You will start by recruiting a core team of individuals to help you flesh out the basics of an action plan. At that point, with a strong sense of what your organization is and what you want to accomplish, you hold a kickoff meeting to gather supporters and put the plan into action.

BUILD YOUR CORE TEAM

Your core team will consist of four to six individuals; these can include students, teachers, faculty members, friends, neighbors, or family. Eventually you'll want people with all sorts of skills in your organization, from fundraising to media outreach to graphic design and more. But for now, find people who follow through on their commitments, are natural-born recruiters (they'll help you grow the organization), and are passionate about your cause. You can probably think of a handful of good candidates already—people with whom you've had great conversations about the issue or close friends who've been antsy to work on an environmental project in your community. Invite those folks to a series of gatherings, where your first goal will be to draft an action plan.

DRAFT YOUR ACTION PLAN

Without a plan, groups can take on aimless projects or activities that don't have clear and tangible results; with one, you can strategically decide where to put your time and energy for the best results. Because a detailed plan provides the foundation for all of your future activities, it is worth the initial investment of group time. To help guide you through the process of developing an action plan, here's a model for students in grades 9–12 who want to implement solar energy on campus. I'll explain each of the components later in this chapter.

➤ SAMPLE ACTION PLAN

Goal: Implement solar energy on campus within two years.

Grade Level: 9–12

Decision Makers: The principal (and possibly the superintendent of schools and/or the school board members).

Strategy: Educate the student body, teachers and staff, and local community members on the benefits of renewable energy on campus, focusing on financial savings and becoming a sustainability leader in the community. Use their support to persuade the administration to install a photovoltaic solar array on campus.

Timeline: 7–24 months

Activism Experience Level: Intermediate: Best for a team with some activist experience or campus with a history of one or more green projects successfully implemented.

➤ MONTH 1

FOCUS	**Educate Yourself and Build Leadership**
MONTHLY ACTION ITEMS	**Delegate leadership** to three fellow students who are going to help you with your campaign. One will coordinate research, one will coordinate viable partners and companies, and one will coordinate outreach to the campus administration. Each of these students should recruit other students to help with their efforts. **Research** the issue. What's feasible in your location? What local, state, or federal credits or taxes exist for your area? Who is the current power provider and where does their energy originate? Have other students in your area (or beyond) successfully implemented a similar project? If so, how?
TIPS	Expressing the **WHY** behind what you are doing is immensely important. Tell it well and the campaign will sell itself. Some potential reasons to install solar? Cost savings, good PR for the campus, sustainability, and educational benefits.

➤ MONTH 2

FOCUS	**Calculate Costs and Feasibility**
MONTHLY ACTION ITEMS	**Ascertain** the level of potential campus administrative support. Ask yourself: Have they funded similar initiatives, green or not, at your campus? How much red tape do you think you'll need to deal with? **Calculate the cost** of implementing a system—ask installation companies to give you a free quote. Calculate energy savings annually and determine the number of years to pay for the system using costs saved. Many energy companies will do the assessment calculations for you.
TIPS	The history of past campus environmental initiatives (both attempts and successes) are often good indicators of potential administrative buy-in. Examine companies to see whether they have successfully worked with campuses before.

➤ MONTH 3

FOCUS	**Choose an Option and Champion Its Adoption**
MONTHLY ACTION ITEMS	**Select your solar energy company.** You don't have to sign on the dotted line, but go forward with the selection of one of your quotes. Select the option that is best and most cost-effective for your situation. The big question: can you raise at least the amount of money quoted for installation?
TIPS	Work with the company that is going to give you the best deal and possible in-kind donations or funding contacts. Make sure the solar energy company will handle any permit fees.

➤ MONTH 3 (continued)

FOCUS	**Educate Your Peers**
MONTHLY ACTION ITEMS	**Build a larger group** of students. Try to get at least ten, as well as a teacher ally that can help you persuade the administration.
TIPS	Try to get a science teacher to back or sponsor your efforts for credibility.
FOCUS	**Admin Meeting**
MONTHLY ACTION ITEMS	**Meet** with your administration. Have a student, a teacher, and a solar energy representative present. Go into the meeting with plenty of facts and exact statistics at the ready. Present the economic benefits first and stress these throughout your presentation. Savings can be quite substantial with solar energy, depending on your location, and this is most likely what your administrator will be most concerned with. Share letters of support from potential funders, parent associations, and other partners.
	Make sure your student leaders are doing their jobs and give them support in preparation for the admin meeting.
TIPS	Prep your administration for the meeting. Give them a one-page summary of your "ask" and benefits, with adequate time for their review. Remember that the campus can predict future revenue from the system's guaranteed savings. This could go to your group for future initiatives or fund more teachers, books, computers, and so on.
FOCUS	**Next Steps**
MONTHLY ACTION ITEMS	**If you are successful,** congrats! One big hurdle crossed. Now it's time to develop a separate fundraising plan. See chapter 9, on fundraising, for ideas.

➤ MONTHS 4–6

FOCUS	**Outreach**
MONTHLY ACTION ITEMS	**If your meeting was unsuccessful,** assess what needs to be done specifically to address the administration's concerns. You may need to build public and student support for the project. Some ideas follow.
TIPS	Keep in mind that you may not win support after one meeting; often it requires long-term discussion. Stay focused on the goal and be persistent!
FOCUS	**Communications**
MONTHLY ACTION ITEMS	**Develop a communications strategy** for your issue and group. Bring in the campus or district's communications officer for help on this. Review chapter 8, Make Media Headlines, for help with messaging and media outreach.

➤ MONTHS 4–6 (continued)

MONTHLY ACTION ITEMS	**Develop a campaign website** that includes as much information as possible for community residents, the campus body and administration, and potential funders. Raise awareness!
TIPS	Continue to thank and support your leaders, volunteers, and funders. Breaks are important, so take your group out for ice cream or pizza as a thank-you for their hard work. A $25 outlay for saying thank-you is a worthy investment.
FOCUS	**Build Support**
MONTHLY ACTION ITEMS	**Pass a resolution** in support of the project through student government. **Hold rallies** or events to raise awareness of your issue on the personal, campus, district, and community level and invite the media. Collect letters of support from community members.
TIPS	Draft a press release with help from your campus's communications team to be sent to media a day or two before the event and on the day.

➤ MONTH 7

FOCUS	**Convince the Administration**
MONTHLY ACTION ITEMS	**Meet again** with the administration once you can demonstrate student, faculty, and parental support for the project and can address any concerns they raised in the first meeting.
FOCUS	**Sign the Contract**
MONTHLY ACTION ITEMS	Repeat public outreach and meetings with administrators until you are successful.
FOCUS	**Installation and Party**
MONTHLY ACTION ITEMS	**Secure the contract** once your funding is adequate. See chapter 9, on fundraising, for ideas. **Host** a day of celebration for you, campus officials, funders, elected officials, and media to take part in the turning on or launching of the system. **Calculate** the emissions and money you have saved with this campaign and send a report to your administration, elected officials, and local media. **Thank** all parties involved. Make them out to be the heroes in this effort.
TIPS	You have momentum! Take a break, but do not wait too long to start a new project or your energized volunteers are likely to move on.

So what are the pieces that make up an action plan? Let's break them down, starting with goals, decision makers, messages, and strategies.

Goals: Dreams with a Deadline

Goals will provide direction and focus to your group. They will keep you and everyone you work with on track, while also providing a way to measure how successful you have been. Goals should be SMART: Specific, Measurable, Achievable, Rewarding, and Timely. The action plan just detailed aims to "implement solar energy on campus within two years." This goal is a *specific* and concrete way to create change (installing solar energy on campus) rather than vague (transitioning our society to a clean energy future). It's *measurable*: students can see the moment at which they have hit their goal when the solar panels are installed on campus. It can be difficult to gauge what's definitely *achievable* from day one, but if a team with some solid previous activism experience embarks on this action plan, or the campus has implemented other environmental initiatives previously, the goal is very likely achievable. It's *rewarding*, as it will make a real difference to the planet (by reducing reliance on dirty energy and by reducing the environmental footprint of the campus). And finally, it's *timely*. Goals are dreams with a deadline, so put an end point on your goal.

In this case, the team members gave themselves a maximum of two years to get solar panels on campus. As you're determining your timeline, think about whether your group is committed to working on this campaign only until a certain date (such as the end of a school year, for campus projects). Is there a specific date by which you absolutely must achieve victory? For example, the city council may be voting on a budget for a development project on a certain date. What are the external factors, such as elections, that could potentially accelerate or slow the progress of your campaign? How much energy and enthusiasm will your group have for doing this work over a longer period of time?

If you're a newly established group, choose initial projects with a short timeline rather than assuming the group will be committed to working together for years. As you are thinking about the timeline for your first project, it's a good time for your core group to discuss the longevity of the organization as a whole. Are you coming together to work on one particular issue or hoping this organization will live on to address other issues after your first success?

Thoughtful goal-setting is crucial: every other part of your action plan flows from having SMART goals, so don't rush through this part of the plan. There's no right or wrong answer to what makes a good goal. It's all dependent on your team, your resources, your community's receptivity to environmental initiatives, and the amount of time you have available to work toward your goal. Here are a few examples of how your group could contribute to the clean energy movement:

> Launch a service to provide energy efficiency improvements to homes in your community

> Convince your campus to purchase renewable energy credits (RECs) to cover 25 percent of the campus's energy usage

> Secure a commitment from the school district to purchase 30 percent of its energy from renewable energy sources within the next five years

> Implement a new clean energy policy on campus

> Work with other local groups to defeat development of a proposed coal-fired power plant

> Advocate for more stringent air-quality regulations for a local power plant

> Lobby for a particular piece of state or federal climate legislation

> Lobby for a local bond to support affordable public transportation

To help your group home in on its goal (and later, its strategies), brainstorm with your core team the answers to the following questions, and capture your ideas on paper:

> How do political, economic, cultural, and other factors contribute to the problem? What -isms (racism, classism, ageism, and so on) may be contributing to the problem? How can you go beyond addressing the symptoms of the problem to addressing the root causes?

> How have other youth across the nation tackled the issue? Are there any youth or student victories that can serve as models for your work?

> If others are working on this issue, how can you help advance or improve a project that's already been started? What can you do that hasn't been done already?

> Are there certain approaches to addressing this issue that would best use your skill set and experience?

> Dream outrageously: of the many potential solutions you've now seen for this environmental challenge, what's the most exciting solution your group could bring to the table?

> Is your solution temporary or permanent? What will happen when you (or your group) move on from the issue?

> How will your group know when it has been successful?

Once you and your core group have settled on a goal, you have to start thinking about how you are going to achieve it. Sometimes you can attain your goal without getting approval or permission from an outside individual. For instance, if you want to launch a community organic garden on city land and you already have a space reserved, you may not need to persuade anyone to give you what you want. You just roll up your sleeves, recruit a team, and get to work! However, if you want to pass legislation or set up some solar panels on the roof of your school, you probably can't do that alone, right? That leads us to the next consideration for our action plan: our decision makers.

Decision Makers

Other people often hold the power to enact your goals, so you need to seek the support of these individuals. Referred to as *targets* or *decision makers*, these key players are the people who will help you succeed or can block your progress. Ask yourself who has formal decision-making power related to your issue.

For the solar power campaign just described, the decision maker is the principal, who ultimately makes big decisions about campus projects.

At some campuses you may also need the buy-in of the superintendent of schools or a majority vote from the local school board members. A decision maker is always a specific individual or a handful of individuals, never a company, an organization, or a group. For example, your decision maker could be three members of congress, but would never be just Congress. If your decision maker is your campus president and the head of campus facilities, you would never describe them as "campus administration." Campus administration actually includes each person working on campus in an administrative capacity—and most of them don't have any power to enact the changes you want to see on campus. It's important to make these distinctions because you should design your entire action plan to convince precisely the people who need convincing, rather than diluting your efforts by talking to lots of people who might support your goals but don't have the power to make them a reality. If you need to win a majority of six votes from a school board consisting of ten individuals, you would identify the six board members most likely to vote yes on your project and focus your outreach efforts on them.

If you've discovered that your group is going to need the support of a decision maker in order to win a victory for your cause, you'll next need to examine not only who has the power to implement your goals, but also what (and who) will persuade those people to take action.

To help you follow the lines of power related to your issue, get together with your core team and brainstorm the answers to these questions:

> What kind of relationship do you have with your decision maker(s)?

> How does your decision maker view your group?

> Do you have any influence over your decision maker(s)?

> Does your decision maker have any vested interest in listening to or working with your group?

As students, you and your group have some influence over campus administrators or faculty. As a voting resident of a town, able to mobilize other voters, you may have some influence with the mayor, and you may have influence with an elected official for your state. As a shopper who has frequented a particular store for years, you may have some influence through your buying power.

Remember Six Degrees of Kevin Bacon, the game in which you can link anyone on the planet to Kevin within six steps? Well, that's a useful concept in action planning, too, for power mapping: the process of figuring out how to influence your decision maker. If you don't have much power or influence over your decision maker, determine who else does—their family members, leaders at their place of worship (such as a rabbi, priest, or pastor), or business colleagues. How can you reach those individuals? You want to bring them onto your team or convince them to exert their influence on your behalf.

Power mapping is a visual exercise: write your decision makers' names on the center of a big piece of paper, then draw links to all the people or groups that influence them. These are your secondary targets. Continue by drawing links to the people who influence the secondary targets. A power map consists of concentric rings of names and groups, and your goal is to figure out how to get access to the inner ring (or as close to it as possible).

I'll talk more about strategies for influencing decision makers later on. The next step in working through your action plan is to choose talking points to encapsulate the key messages you want to publicly convey about your campaign.

Message: Know Your Audience

Talking points help you distill a complex issue into a handful of clear and simple phrases about the problem and solution. Ideally, the messages you develop will speak to many different audiences, from the general public to your peers and the decision makers, but sometimes you may want to develop different messages for each one of these groups.

For example, if you're working on campus to install solar panels, think about what your campus administration cares about most: is it cost savings, being seen as a leader in the community or the state, or taking the lead from the student body? Your key message will be completely different if your campus cares more about cost savings than about being seen as a leader. Your message to the teachers may differ, too: you may emphasize the teaching opportunities that new solar panels would provide. And your message to the student body probably won't talk about cost savings: how many students are interested in saving their campus money? Instead, you might talk about how leadership in this effort will give students great experience to help them stand out during college application time or how it will give them a leg up in the emerging green economy after graduation.

Make sure that everyone working on your core team helps develop the key messages, understands them, and is prepared to repeat (and expound on) them. If you're working outside of campus to influence a business, ask your team the same questions. What does the business tout as its strength: is it quality products, being an industry leader, value and low prices, or community involvement and engagement? Again, you can tailor your message depending on what the company leaders tout as their priorities. For an elected official, your message might be totally different during an election year (when they're vulnerable to negative publicity) from your message during an off-year. If the official is planning to leave office, your message might be focused on what legacy this leader plans to leave behind.

Once you have your messaging down, it's time to think about how you're going to achieve your goals.

Strategy

There are many different strategies for creating change on any issue. Here's a brief description of a handful of the most common ones:

- ➤ Advocacy: Persuading decision makers to make changes through public pressure, stepping into a decision-making position yourself (student council member, youth representative on a campus board of directors), or creating a new decision-making body representing youth.

- ➤ Education: Raising awareness in the public, with the goal of asking people to change their behaviors or lobby decision makers, for example.

- ➤ Providing goods and services: Directly providing a needed good or service to individuals or groups, such as installing energy-efficient lightbulbs in residential settings or establishing an organic food kitchen for the homeless.

> Fundraising: Raising funds for groups already doing great work or investing in products or services to meet an environmental need.

> Litigation: Suing companies or institutions at fault.

> Nonviolent direct action: Drawing attention to your issue and pressuring decision makers to make change, using confrontational tactics.

Evaluate how successful each of these strategies (and others you can think of) might be for hitting your goals. In the case of the solar campaign, the strategy is a combination of education and advocacy:

"Educate the student body, teachers and staff, and local community members on the benefits of renewable energy on campus, focusing on financial savings and becoming a sustainability leader in the community. Use their support to persuade the administration to install a photovoltaic solar array on campus."

Let's evaluate the other strategies mentioned above in light of the goal: implement solar energy on campus within two years. You can't provide goods or services on campus without the buy-in of the administration. Even if you could raise all of the funds to install the system, you will still need the sign-on from the administration—you can't just hire a company to show up one day and install the system. You'll have to persuade your administration that it's a good idea, using advocacy and educational outreach techniques. Nonviolent direct action or litigation would be unnecessary; you don't need to protest or sue the campus! Those strategies are typically best used when your decision maker is squarely opposed to implementing your action plan. So a combination of education and advocacy is a good choice for this goal.

Now you've got the major elements of your action plan: the goal, the decision maker, and the strategies to implement your goal. You'll select your tactics soon—the specific actions you're going to take—but before you do, it's good to understand the resources you have at your disposal and how you can use those resources to influence your decision makers.

Key Players: Your Friends, Your Soon-to-Be Friends, and the Thorns in Your Side

People are your greatest resource (and they can also pose your biggest challenges!). Key players fall into two camps: allies, the people or groups you can collaborate with to work toward victory, and opponents, the people or groups fighting against you.

To figure out who your key players are, get your core group together and brainstorm. Start by listing the individuals who can help you achieve victory. Who else is affected by the cause you are working on? Are there specific community members, scientists, lawyers, doctors, parents, academics and professors, religious leaders, politicians, or groups toward whom you should direct outreach and recruitment? What reporters and media contacts or potential funders do you have access to? Who else is already working on this issue: groups, individuals, companies, elected officials? If you are a student, what student groups, academic departments, or administrative units would support your campaign?

For the solar campaign, here are potential allies:

➤ Your environmental science teacher: Renewable energy is a huge part of environmental science, and having a renewable energy resource right on the campus would be a tremendous educational tool for this teacher.

➤ Parent associations, like the PTA: If your administration is on the fence, tap into these involved and dedicated parents.

➤ The local energy company: If you can arrange a meeting with them, do so. You may be able to talk your way into a reduced-price solar panel system.

➤ Local businesses: Find local businesses run by the parents of your peers. They would be a great asset to reach out to during fundraising drives. You might also be able to convince them to use renewable energy in their own buildings.

➤ Any environmental, outdoors, service clubs, or social justice clubs on your campus, besides your own: They may help you with your renewable energy campaign.

➤ Local philanthropy clubs: Dedicated adults love to help out dedicated youth—try Rotary Clubs and other service and philanthropy groups.

While you'll have plenty of allies, you may also have some opponents. Who might oppose your campaign? How might they challenge you? How much time, money, and energy do you think they will invest? What are their strengths and weaknesses? What can you do to neutralize their opposition? Once you've answered these questions, you're ready to move on to developing tactics—the portion of your action plan that makes you visible to the outside world.

Tactics: Going Public

Tactics are the individual actions, events, and activities your group hosts to advance your goals. Sometimes people confuse goals and tactics. Goals are outcomes; tactics are the methods and tools you use to achieve those outcomes. For example, if your goal is to install solar panels on campus, one tactic can be hosting a campus teach-in on renewable energy. Actions, events, and activities shouldn't be the goals in and of themselves; rather, they are ways to reach your bigger goal. That's why you should always choose your goal first and then identify your tactics. Otherwise you might get caught up in planning a flashy demonstration or fundraiser without analyzing whether it will really help you reach your ultimate goal.

In addition to being strategic, tactics should be fun for your group, raise the morale of your members, and demonstrate your power in a way that brings more people, resources, and media attention to your cause.

Let's look at the tactics from the solar campaign. The first months are devoted to researching the best solar company for the campus and assessing the potential level of administrative support; then the plan dives into education and advocacy. The initial tactic is to host a meeting with the administrators, present the plan, and seek their support. If that fails, it's time for education and building support. Educational tactics include conducting media outreach for the issue and group as well as developing a campaign website. Once the group has done more campus education, it can incorporate additional advocacy tactics, including:

➤ passing a resolution in support of the project through student government,

➤ holding rallies or events to raise awareness of the issue on the personal, campus, district, and community level (be sure to invite the media!), and,

➤ collecting letters of support from community members.

As soon as the group can demonstrate abundant student, faculty, and parental support for the project, group members will meet again with the administration.

Once your core group has brainstormed a list of tactics, go down the list, evaluating each tactic with this question: "Does this tactic align with our strategy to convince the decision maker to adopt our goal?" If the answer is yes, it's an appropriate tactic. If the answer is no, cross this tactic off your list.

If you're having a hard time coming up with appropriate tactics, here are some more ideas:

➤ Join a policy-making body to represent the student voice

➤ Create and deliver photo petitions in which people hold signs expressing their opinions

➤ Organize a group of peers to attend and speak at a school board meeting

➤ Hold a forum discussion

➤ Create your own documentary

➤ Moderate school debates or organize a campus-wide assembly

➤ Conduct a poster and art outreach campaign or create an eco-mural on campus

➤ Organize a spoken word performance or poetry night

➤ Set up interviews with local newspapers and radio stations

To learn about tactics that you can adapt for your own campaign, read the case studies of successful efforts from groups mentioned in chapter 1, such as the Sierra Student Coalition and the Energy Action Coalition. Reading the chapter on tactics in *Organizing for Social Change: Midwest Academy Manual for Activists* can also be helpful (see the resources at the end of this chapter).

When you are choosing your tactics, remember that they can run the gamut, from cooperation with your decision maker to engaging in conflict. Writing a letter to the editor praising your state senator as an eco-champion and calling on her to sign a new bill to improve fuel-efficiency standards for vehicles statewide—well, that's on the cooperative side of things. Writing a letter that attacks the state senator for slacking off on environmental issues and not yet signing onto the bill—that's using confrontation. The same tactics—meetings, press outreach, rallies, public forums—can be approached from the perspective of either working with your decision makers (or gently nudging them to embrace your demands) or launching an all-out attack, putting them on the spot.

Carefully decide whether you want to work in cooperation with or against your decision maker. Both can be effective, but make sure that you think about the consequences of your actions for the group in the future. How will other individuals and groups view your group in light of the tactics you choose to use? Be careful when choosing tactics that could alienate your decision makers. If they're already squarely opposed to your demands, you might start with confrontational tactics. However, if your decision maker has traditionally been eco-friendly or is on the fence on this particular issue, you probably want to start with cooperative tactics. It's always easier to move toward more confrontational tactics later in the game than it is to try to collaborate after initially being aggressive.

Once you've developed a list of tactics, it's time to place them into a timeline.

Timeline: Working Backward

In what might feel like a contradiction, you'll start at the end of your action plan and work backward as you create a timeline. Start with the end goal; for example, "solar panels installed within two years." On a huge piece of paper or a board, write your end goal ("panels installed") at the far right end of a line, which will become your timeline.

The solar panels action plan allotted a minimum of seven months for the campaign, but took into account that it could take up to two years. This action plan requires fundraising to achieve the end goal, so that became the focus of the second year. The focus during the first year was to get the administration to agree to the panels. If you are working on a campus project, remember that you have only about seven or eight months available during the school year for organizing. You'll want to wrap everything up before the last month of school, when finals and graduation will become all-consuming for many students and the administration.

Working backward, plot each one of your tactics on your timeline. To evaluate whether or not your timeline is reasonable, estimate the amount of time each tactic will take to pull off, from planning to execution and follow-up. Many tactics can be broken into component parts. For example, if you want to collect letters from the campus student body, you'll have to:

1. Draft a sample text
2. Develop an outreach plan
3. Collect the letters
4. Sort and package them for delivery
5. Deliver the letters to your decision maker

Each of these steps takes time. Guesstimate how much time it will take for each step (and be generous). Then double that estimate—or if this is your first time trying this tactic, even triple it. Just about every step will take longer than you originally plan. Doubling your estimate allows for the flake factor of volunteers, unforeseen obstacles, and other things that will slow your implementation.

Write down next to each tactic the number of hours you think it will take. Create a separate sticky note for each component of your major tactics and place these on the timeline, too. You may see that one week you've planned sixty hours of work for your team—which may or may not be reasonable. Because your tactics are written on a sticky note, you can shift them around easily, until you find what seems like an achievable timeline. Your timeline should be realistic—don't burn yourself out in the beginning—and should account for periods of low activity (for students, that would include campus breaks, midterms, and finals).

When it's all finished, copy the timeline to a permanent document that you can save and review during your meetings. Fixed dates add an urgency to take action now, and they allow you to assess your progress over time.

NEXT STOP: BUILD A GREEN MOVEMENT

You're finished with your action plan! As you've done with the timeline, record your action plan in a permanent document that you can save and review during meetings. Replicate the format of the sample action plan provided earlier in this chapter. If you prefer more structure, you can use action planning worksheets; groups like Youth Venture provide these as free downloads (see Resources). Whatever format you choose, you will share this plan with your peers, potential funders, volunteers, and allies as all of you proceed with the campaign, so that everyone is on the same page.

In the next chapter we'll talk about what it takes to grow your movement or, if you are working with an existing organization, to expand that group even more. It's time to start recruiting!

RESOURCES

The Change Agency, www.thechangeagency.org The Change Agency provides online training resources focusing on tactics, strategy and big-picture thinking, organizational development and maintenance, and personal development and life skills.

Organizing for Social Change: Midwest Academy Manual for Activists, fourth edition, by Kim Bobo, Jackie Kendall, and Steve Max. Santa Ana, CA: The Forum Press, 2010.

The School of Unity and Liberation (SOUL), www.schoolofunity andliberation.org SOUL provides abundant resources for youth looking to identify the root causes of (and possible solutions for) environmental and social problems. SOUL supports the development of a new generation of organizers rooted in a systemic change analysis—particularly youth from marginalized communities.

Youth Venture, www.youthventure.org Youth Venture is a global network of young people creating and leading positive social change. The organization helps teams design and launch their own lasting social ventures. When a Venture team is ready to launch, Youth Venture offers seed funding of up to $1,000, plus guidance, tools, and support.

03
BUILD A GREEN MOVEMENT

RECRUIT PEOPLE TO YOUR CAUSE

O nce you've got an action plan in place, it's time to grow your movement. You are surrounded by people hungry for ways to make an impact in your community and beyond—this chapter is all about how to build a movement of individuals to champion your cause and make change. And if you're working with an existing group, this chapter will teach you the skills you need to expand the group and develop new leaders. Let's start with building a group from scratch.

STARTING A GROUP FROM SCRATCH

Before you start recruiting members for your organization, there are a couple of issues that your core group should think through, including your group's mission statement, the leadership structure, and the decision-making process. Although you can solicit the larger group's feedback on these issues, it's smart to at least have proposals for each of these areas as you go into your first meeting.

➤ Your core group should draft a mission statement—one or two
sentences that states who you are, your vision, and how you plan to
achieve it. If your mission is to "create green jobs," your mission is
still too vague—get specific. Here's a sample: "Teens for Safe Cosmetics is a coalition led by dynamic and passionate young women.
We educate our peers and the public at large about safe and healthy
lifestyle choices that foster healthier homes, schools, and community environments free from harmful chemicals and pollutants."

➤ Who will be responsible for what in the group? Will you elect specific roles, like president, vice president, secretary, and treasurer? Or
do you want a flat structure with no formal hierarchy of leadership
roles? Will you set up a structure in which people alternate roles
each week, like meeting facilitator and meeting organizer?

➤ Will you make decisions by majority vote? Voting is fast, but means
that not everyone in the group may agree on your conclusions.
By consensus? Consensus means that everyone in the group must
agree; the objections of one individual can hold up group process.
At the same time, gaining consensus ensures you're more likely to
have everyone's buy-in. What about committees? These smaller
groups can move forward on projects independently.

Once you've got your plan of action, it's time to tell the world! You'll
want to launch your group with a kickoff meeting. The core group that
helped you develop the action plan will be responsible for helping to formal-
ize your new group and plan your first meeting. If you launch a group on
campus, find out how you can officially register your group, how to access
any available funding, and how to reserve rooms for meetings. On college
and university campuses, the office of student life or student organizations
can provide this information. On high school campuses, find a teacher to
sponsor the group; he or she can provide answers to these questions.

Community groups won't need formal sponsors, but you will need to
find a regular meeting space. Many towns have social justice or community
centers that offer free or low-cost meeting spaces, advertising for upcoming meetings and events, and basic administrative support to newly formed
grassroots groups. In addition, libraries often provide free meeting spaces,

and nonprofits, community foundations, or businesses may make their facilities available after hours.

THE KICKOFF MEETING

The kickoff meeting is your opportunity to get people excited about the work. It should be interactive and welcoming and should hint at the big victories to come after diving into the action plan. With the help of your core team, you should be able to plan a successful kickoff meeting in just three or four weeks.

First, set the date, time, and location for your kickoff meeting that is likely to draw the most people. Host the kickoff meeting in a room that you think you can pack with attendees—it's pretty discouraging to have a mostly empty room for your first meeting. Next, start thinking about publicity.

Get the Word Out

Why would people want to join your group? You've already thought about how your issue connects with your fellow youth, so use that information to make a list of potential supporters. Brainstorm every person you know who might want to join you and reach out with a personal invitation—in person or by phone. Get tech-y. Advertise the meeting using Twitter, text messages, and updates to your social networking sites. After you've invited everyone you know, reach beyond your personal circles. Advertising executives say that seven is the magic number: people need to hear a message seven times before it begins to sink in. So don't worry about oversaturating your campus or community with your message—that's the best way to ensure a great turnout!

To publicize your kickoff meeting, try some or all of the following ideas. For meetings on campus:

> ➤ Table tents: Table tents are advertisements printed on pieces of paper folded in half (like a tent) to stand upright. Set them on tables in the dining hall, library, or other places where students congregate. It's a good idea to get approval from Dining Services or the library staff, so they don't remove your notices!

➤ Class announcements: Get permission to make a short, upbeat announcement in classes or at extracurricular gatherings. Send around a signup sheet or 3 x 5 cards to capture the contact details of interested folks; for big classes, 3 x 5 cards are quickest—you don't have to wait for one signup sheet to make its way around a classroom. Pass out the cards in advance of your talk, and ask people to fill out their info on the card at the end if they're interested. Follow up within twenty-four hours by phone or email with more details on how to get involved.

➤ Chalk drawings: Bust out with your artistic talent and draw your own advertisements for your group, along with the 411: date, time, and place for the upcoming meetings. Many campuses allow chalk drawings, but you can check with Student Services if you have any doubts.

➤ PA system: If your school has a centralized PA system with daily announcements, get onto the agenda.

➤ Campus online lists and calendar: Post your upcoming meeting on the online campus calendar and on campus email lists for relevant departments.

For off-campus/community meetings:

➤ Visuals: Place posters and flyers in highly visible places—college campuses, coffee shops, libraries, community centers, bulletin boards. Post in designated areas or ask for permission to post, if you're unsure. It's a bummer to spend the time and money on printing up a bunch of flyers, only to have them taken down because you didn't have permission to post. Create posters that people can read from twenty feet away: visuals are key, and you should limit text to the important details, like the time, place, and location for your meetings. Think of unconventional places to post, like bathroom stalls, where you have a captive audience.

➤ Media: Place ads or notices in campus or community news outlets: newspapers, television, or radio.

> Tabling: Pass out information and talk to individuals on campuses
> or in front of busy shopping areas. You can distribute more than a
> hundred leaflets in an hour in busy areas. You can also stop people
> to ask them to sign a petition or postcard (remember to bring
> pens!)—giving you an opportunity for a short conversation. Catch
> people's attention with an invitation: "Do you have thirty seconds
> to help clean up our community's air?" Then hand them a postcard,
> and while they're filling it out, invite them to your group's meeting.

After you've done a thorough job of advertising, it's time to rock your
first meeting so people want to come back.

Tips for a Successful Kickoff Meeting

Sitting through a boring, poorly facilitated, frustrating, or too-long meeting is a drag—and can dampen someone's enthusiasm for getting involved
with your group. First impressions count! The biggest piece of advice I can
give is to have fun. Build in time for socializing during each meeting. All
work and no play can make for a very dreary group. Plan for refreshments,
and advertise the food and drink. Everybody loves to eat. Local restaurants
and grocery stores are likely to give free donations, if you ask with enough
advance notice (often three to four weeks). You'll find that offering food
draws more individuals. Once they're in the room, it's your job to get them
excited about the issues.

Set an agenda in advance to focus the discussion and add suggested
times to each agenda item. Include time for announcements. Effective
meetings typically run thirty to sixty minutes, plus time to socialize or
break into working groups. Put the most important issues at the beginning
of the agenda in case you have to cut a meeting short, and post the agenda
in a prominent place at the start of each meeting.

Honor people's time constraints by beginning and ending meetings
when you said you would. Start with introductions. Introductions give
everyone in the room an opportunity to speak in the first ten minutes of
the meeting, and help people loosen up. Shifting from introductions to ice-
breakers or games at the start of the meeting gets strangers talking to one
another and helps encourage shy newcomers to break out of their shells
early—making their participation later in the meeting more likely.

SAMPLE KICKOFF MEETING AGENDA

7:00–7:10	Welcome and group introductions
7:10–7:15	Icebreaker or game
7:15–7:18	Review agenda and introduce the facilitator, note taker, and time-keeper to attendees
7:18–7:25	Briefing on the issue and the group's origin
7:25–7:40	Introduce action plan; questions and answers
7:40–7:50	Develop group agreements
7:50–8:00	Announcements
8:00–8:30	Working groups breakout
8:30–9:00	Establishment of next meeting time, date, and location before pizza (remember vegan options!) and socializing
9:00	Close up the room and say good-byes

Set group agreements. Also called *ground rules*, agreements are a set of guidelines to ensure productive and respectful meetings and group interactions. Sample agreements could include the following:

➤ Arrive on time, start on time, and finish on time, as much as possible.

➤ If you make a commitment, follow through. If you can't fulfill your commitment, let someone know well before any deadlines.

➤ Don't interrupt when others are speaking.

➤ Don't use sexist, racist, homophobic, or other disrespectful language.

➤ Respect diversity of ideas.

Brainstorm agreements during the first meeting, and post them for all successive meetings. If someone breaks a group agreement down the line, the facilitator can challenge the behavior, not the person. For more information about setting group agreements, see the resources at the end of the chapter.

Select an individual to facilitate the meeting and a timekeeper to watch the clock and keep the group on track. Look at the gender dynamics at play when people volunteer for roles and work toward gender equality, so females aren't always taking notes while males are facilitating the meetings. Many group members won't know much about your group's issue. Provide an overview of the issue and the origin of your group. This is a great place to share results from the research and action planning stages of your work and your opportunity to make sure that everyone is on the same page about the group's goals and mission. Listen to others' opinions about the mission statement. If they understand and support the vision, approve it and move forward; if not, capture their suggestions and work on a revised statement in a smaller subgroup. This is a good time for people who drastically disagree with what you and your planning group have decided to work toward to move on to another organization—though if you've got a huge group and the capacity to tackle multiple action plans, you can decide to do that, too.

Create working groups. Sometimes it's easier to get everyone involved when you break into small groups of three to seven individuals, each group focused on a different task or project. Choose a few pieces of your action plan—things that don't require a ton of planning or expertise—for your group to start working on during the first meeting. This might include, for example, some of the tactics from your action plan focused on education and outreach, such as an educational movie night, a one-day tree planting project, a guided tour of green businesses, or research and fundraising. These initial projects give people a way to get educated and take action on your cause immediately. Once people are involved in something concrete, they are more likely to come back to the next meeting and the meeting after that.

Take minutes. Notes, or minutes, serve as a record of what was decided, who volunteered for specific tasks, and more. Notes can also be sent to individuals who miss the meeting, to keep them in the loop. Be sure to leave each meeting with next steps, a timeline for action items, and a person assigned to each task. In addition to minutes, pass around sign-in sheets, or get individuals to fill out a 3 x 5 card with their contact details, so you can follow up with attendees after the meeting.

Everyone should leave knowing the date, time, and place for the next meeting. Weekly or bimonthly meetings are best—if you meet just once a month, there's too much time in between the meetings to make real progress. Ideally, the most excited individuals will leave with specific tasks to work on, such as research or fundraising, so they can already begin

STYLES OF PARTICIPATION AND LISTENING

The facilitator's role is to draw out the perspectives of as many group members as possible—not to do most of the talking—so someone who is a respectful communicator and sensitive to group dynamics is key. The facilitator also makes sure to welcome fresh ideas in brainstorms. By definition, in these sessions you don't shoot down any ideas, but add all of the suggestions to the pot; later the group can debate the merits of each. Criticizing ideas during a brainstorm only serves to stifle the discussion.

The facilitator pays attention to who speaks and who doesn't and offers the model of "step up, step back"; if certain individuals are speaking too frequently, they should "step back" to open an opportunity for others to share. The facilitator makes sure that no one person dominates the meeting. If other folks are quiet, they should be encouraged to "step up" and contribute.

Here are some strategies for facilitators to ensure that the group hears from all of the voices in the room.

POPCORN: People speak out as they have an idea, going around the room. All suggestions are noted without comment or criticism.

DYADS OR TRIADS: Break into smaller groups of two or three people. Assign time limits for each individual to speak and share impressions, or allow for a free-flowing discussion. Capture the best ideas generated during the breakout to report back to the larger group.

SHARING CIRCLE: Going around in a circle, everyone takes turns in sharing, with no interruptions. A "talking stick" or other item can be used to help hold the space for the individual who is sharing. To keep a conversation rolling, you can use time limits or an hourglass.

NONVERBAL PARTICIPATION: To get a quick show of support or opposition for a proposal, you can ask for a show of hands or thumbs-up/down.

ASKING FOR NEW VOICES: The facilitator can explicitly ask to hear only from individuals who have not yet spoken.

contributing to the group. Reiterate action steps the group decided on and dates for completion.

Meeting Follow-Up

After the kickoff meeting, make sure your core team stays around for at least fifteen minutes to debrief. A debrief is a discussion after an event by the core planning group that reflects on strengths, areas for improvement, and next steps. It's a good idea to start debriefing after all of your big meetings and actions.

Here are some sample questions for debriefs:

➤ How was the group participation?

➤ What worked well with the facilitation, and what needs improvement?

➤ What ideas emerged from the group?

➤ Did we follow our agenda, and if not, was our departure productive?

➤ What were the highlights of the gathering?

➤ Do we feel like the next steps will help us achieve our goals?

After a debrief, you can set the draft agenda for the next meeting, choose the new facilitator, and divvy up planning tasks.

Once you've hosted a successful kickoff meeting, you and your team will be primed and ready to start working for your cause. However, before you hit the ground running, take a few minutes to read the following sections about how to build and maintain a healthy organization.

GOOD PRACTICES FOR HEALTHY ORGANIZATIONS

So many groups are launched with the best intentions and then fizzle out or even break apart over disagreements that could have been avoided. When you use best practices with your team, and within the larger campus or community, you send a message to everyone that you take your work seriously and that your organization is here to stay.

Recruit and Retain Volunteers

You and your core planning group don't have time to be responsible for everything that your organization does. The best way to grow new leaders and get people invested in your action plan is to give them a way to pitch in.

One of the classic challenges of campus organizing is the reality that talented leaders leave (and students graduate) each year. To grow a lasting team, work on building the leadership capacity of younger leaders year-round. That way, when your core team members move on, the group won't fold. Cultivating a leadership ladder with rungs of advancing responsibility is one key to growing a larger movement of talented activists and ensuring your group's strength. It may seem easier to reserve the important tasks for yourself and your friends. However, people are more likely to stay involved with your group if you offer them some challenges and ways to contribute meaningfully.

Here's an example of how to do this: a new activist shows up at a meeting. You invite her to join the working committee for an upcoming rally. During that breakout group, you make sure she leaves with a specific role: perhaps she's to partner with someone else to invite the speakers. Someone from your core team checks in with her regularly in the month leading up to the event, and after the rally you meet with her to talk about what went well, what (if anything) could be improved, and what her next leadership responsibility could be.

Make a list of all responsibilities for an event or meeting, and let people step up to the plate. Check in regularly on the progress of each individual organizer: it can help to have a written checklist of tasks. If someone says, "I've got it covered," don't be afraid to ask specific questions: exactly what progress has the person made to date, and what remains? Volunteers do flake out, despite their best intentions. If someone isn't making progress on their tasks, don't be afraid to reallocate jobs and find a better fit for them in another volunteer role more suited to their interests, time, and strengths.

That said, everyone makes mistakes; it's how we grow as activists (and humans!). As a good leader, you have to allow people to take risks and sometimes fail. If they fail repeatedly, well, it's probably not a good idea to give them additional leadership roles without some strong coaching and a partner with more experience. But occasional hiccups? That's natural, and no reason to shut people out of the leadership ladder.

Another way to expand your group is by offering valuable training opportunities, like workshops.

Host Trainings

Rather than learning entirely by trial-and-error, invite a trainer or professional to host a workshop focused on activist skills, environmental issues, or both. People love growing their knowledge base and skills, so trainings are a great way to recruit and retain group members. Plus, training your team gives you a better shot at successfully implementing your action plan—and people like to be a part of a winning team.

Some national groups will train youth in your community for free or at a low cost, such as the Sierra Student Coalition (www.ssc.org). Others offer web-based or telephone training if they can't travel to join you in person. Discover who is doing good work in the community, and ask them whether they'd be willing to impart their skills to your crew. Many paid and volunteer staff from community-based and regional environmental groups would be happy to share their skill set and knowledge—and they may become new allies for your campaign! You may even be able to look to students or teachers in your community to provide activist and issues training.

Follow these steps to plan a strong training for your group.

1. ESTABLISH YOUR GOAL.

Before you invite a workshop trainer, get clear on what you want from the training. Precisely what skills training and knowledge does your group seek? How much time do you have available—two hours, a whole day, or a weekend? How many individuals do you realistically expect to show up? Set a budget for the event, including facilities, food, materials, and trainer compensation, if any.

2. FIND THE RIGHT TRAINER(S).

Brainstorm a list of trainers, and start interviewing them about their training topics and style. There are many different learning styles: some people learn by watching, others by listening, and others by hands-on activities. The best trainings usually incorporate all of these learning styles as well as plenty of role-plays. Role-plays are participatory exercises in which you might, for example, practice pitching a news story to a reporter, or do a mock meeting with a business owner to ask for financial support. Ask trainers for references, and follow up with them. A great activist is not necessarily a good trainer. Do your homework before selecting one or more trainers that you think are the best fit for your group.

3. ORGANIZE YOUR LOGISTICS.

Ask the trainer what size and layout of space is best, and reserve space accordingly. Put together a materials list—both materials that the trainer will need (possibly a projector and computer, flip charts, markers, or whiteboards) and materials the participants will need (things like pens, paper, and nametags). It can be helpful to draft a statement of expectations for the trainer, including information like event date and time, payment, materials provided, and responsibilities of the trainer and the group.

4. RECRUIT, RECRUIT, RECRUIT.

If you're paying for training, you want to get the biggest bang for the buck. If a trainer is volunteering time, you want to honor that contribution with a decent crowd of trainees. Either way, recruit everyone you know to the training, not just folks from your own group. Consider opening it up to community members or students at nearby campuses. Require people to fill out some kind of registration form rather than simply making a verbal commitment; people who make even a small advance payment, like $5 (to help cover food costs, if not training costs), are more likely to show up.

5. TRAIN AWAY.

Bring paper and pens for people to take notes and lots of snacks and drinks to keep people's energy high. Arrive in advance to set up the room (chairs, tables, flip charts, and so on) as the trainer has requested. It's helpful to have at least one person present whose entire responsibility is dealing with logistics and assisting the trainer rather than participating in the training.

6. DEBRIEF AND THANKS.

After the trainer leaves, evaluate the training: does your group feel more prepared to tackle your action plan? What went well, and what could be improved? Feel free to share this feedback with the trainer, along with a sincere thank-you.

THE LAW OF HALVES

The law of halves is a great tool to estimate attendance, participation, donations, and more. For example, if you're planning an evening film screening, the law of halves says you can pretty accurately estimate the number of individuals that will show. You can start with the signup lists you have gathered from meetings, class talks, and tabling. Let's say you begin with eighty names; the law of halves indicates that half of those individuals—forty people—would agree to come to your event if you called or emailed them to ask them personally. Out of those forty who said yes, twenty would actually show on the day of the event. So to get about twenty people to an event, you should call or personally ask about eighty individuals to attend. Don't take it personally when people don't show—maybe something came up with their friends or family, they're not feeling well, or they had to work at the last minute. If you use the law of halves, you'll expect some attrition and won't be disappointed.

Be Organized

Don't wait until the day you graduate to write down everything the next leadership team needs to manage the organization. Keep track of the following information, ideally in some shared online system so all of the members of your core team have access and can update the documents regularly.

➤ You should already have your action plan recorded, but update it regularly.

➤ Record contact information for key players (both allies and non-allies) with notes about the history of the relationships and anything else a new person might need to know.

➤ Compile a list of free places to host events and meetings, along with
contact information for the people who can help you set them up.

➤ Take notes after every big event you host; this evaluation will be
particularly helpful for future generations of activists who try to
replicate your success (or improve upon any failures!).

➤ Keep a secure list of passwords for your campaign's social networking or other accounts.

Challenge Oppression

Many groups collapse due to internal strife between individuals or an
inability to work well with outside groups because of the "isms"—destructive ways of creating or supporting inequalities between individuals or
groups based on things like age, skin color, culture, wealth, sexual orientation, gender, and more. Although we've made a lot of progress in combating
these issues, we still have a long way to go. To do good work on green issues
for the long haul, we need to be aware of how our work intersects with
other struggles. All of the issues under the banner of social change are inter-
related. If you are working on cleaning up air pollution, you already know
that it's an environmental issue, a health issue, and most likely a social justice, class, and race issue, too (because many polluting sites are located in
low-income communities).

To make sure that you are taking the "isms" into account and challenging oppression at all levels of your organization, here are some suggestions
for learning more. This is tricky stuff, particularly for individuals embark-
ing on an anti-oppression analysis for the first time. Check out tools for
diversity and combating oppression at Training for Change (www.training
forchange.org) for suggested exercises and conversations you can introduce
to your group. You can also take these steps:

➤ Have each member of your core planning committee research a
system of oppression and then meet to discuss what you can do to
challenge these injustices in your own work arena.

➤ As you learn about the historical struggles of communities and
individuals that have been on the receiving end of injustice and

oppression, see whether you can find the overlap with your group's struggles for the environment.

➤ Examine the privileges and resources you may enjoy as a result of your wealth, skin color, ethnicity, religion, sexuality, and gender. How can you use your privilege and resources to support movements that are working for equality for all peoples?

➤ Work in solidarity with individuals and communities directly affected by the environmental issues you want to address. Take your lead from those communities, support their existing efforts, and ask them for feedback on your action plan. Seek out partners across social, economic, and racial boundaries.

➤ Challenge racist, homophobic, or sexist comments, and create a space during your meetings, actions, and events in which everyone is encouraged to listen, speak, and act with respect.

➤ Speak using "I" statements and do not generalize your own personal experience for others. The Center for Nonviolent Communication (www.cnvc.org) offers tools to help people articulate their personal experience authentically, including speaking from the "I" point of view.

Practicing respectful communication and working well within your team—despite any differences in age, skin color, culture, wealth, sexual orientation, and gender—will position you to build coalitions with different groups in your community.

Foster Coalitions

A coalition is an alliance of individuals or organizations that collaborate to win a particular campaign or to create social change. Coalitions may be permanent or temporary, based around a collection of issues (like sustainable urban development in your downtown) or a single issue (like stopping the construction of a new chain coffee shop). Although solid coalitions take a lot of energy and time to build and maintain, they have more power to make long-term changes than individual groups do.

Working well with individuals from backgrounds that are different from your own can help you build successful coalitions among groups with what may seem to be disparate goals. In the following story, check out how Jessian Choy brought together a surprising coalition to work for the environment.

SUCCESS STORY
LISTEN QUIETLY, SPEAK LOUDLY In 2001, Jessian

Choy was attending the University of California at Santa Cruz (UCSC), where a number of fragmented organizations lacked a collective voice with which to influence administrators to green the campus. Jessian realized that she could accomplish more if she could convince everyone to work together. So at age twenty-one she started the Student Environmental Center (SEC). Jessian's group reached out to student organizations that until then had believed environmentalism was just about saving trees. Jessian's group began by showing members of other groups how they were all working toward the same goal of social justice. For example, promoting organic foods in the dining halls meant that workers in the field would be exposed to fewer toxic chemicals. As a result of her group's outreach, for the first time at UCSC, fifty-five managers, faculty, and students came together to create a comprehensive environmental strategic plan. The diverse coalition of student leaders successfully advocated for UCSC to reduce pesticide use and waste and to increase public transit, green purchasing, and green building practices.

© Leilani Lumen

"Some people say that if you **STAND UP FOR WHAT YOU BELIEVE IN**, people will listen to you. I believe that if you **ALSO LISTEN QUIETLY** to what other people have to say, they will often stand up for what you believe in." **—JESSIAN CHOY**

When you start to build coalitions with other campus groups, be sensitive to the fact that most groups already have full plates. Rather than recruit them away from their existing projects, explore where your issues might dovetail. If you are hosting a rally and hope that the Social Justice Committee will send some of their students, make sure you attend their events or offer some support in return. You scratch my back and I'll scratch yours, right? That helps make both of our campaigns stronger.

In addition to creating local coalitions, check out groups from other campuses. Many of them may be working on the same things that you are and would be more than happy to share their experience with you or work with you to achieve an even larger goal. Multigenerational coalitions are also important. Parents, campus faculty and staff, school board members, local politicians, business leaders, and other adults can be crucial allies to move your work forward.

Evaluate Your Progress

Remember, people power is all about, well, people! You've got to keep the people in your group happy and growing as activists. One of the best ways to make sure you're doing this is evaluation. Build in time regularly during your meetings for people to share how they feel about the group dynamics and the effectiveness (and fun!) of the meetings. And of course you should evaluate your team's progress on your action plan. Here are some helpful questions to pose to the group regarding your action plan:

> Have you met any of your goals? Has your decision maker expressed any interest in or commitments to helping you implement your goals? Have you spoken with other individuals and groups affected by this issue, to gauge their impressions of your work?

> What tactics have been successful, to date? Why? If they weren't successful, what could you have done differently? Is your messaging well received when you execute your tactics?

> Is your team working well together? Have you increased the size of your team? Do you have support from more people now than when you started?

And beware of forming a clique of insiders. Between group meetings, members of your core team should take the time to meet individually with newcomers. You can find out more about their interests and what they'd like to contribute to the group. Although email is quick and ideal for announcements and reminders, personal contact is always best to build strong relationships and to really show each new group member that he or she matters.

NEXT STOP: SPREAD YOUR MESSAGE

So you've established an action plan and formed a powerhouse group. What's next? People can't get engaged until they get informed. If you don't share the news about your issue, maybe no one else will. The next chapter will help you spread the word about your group and issue and build peer and public support for your projects.

RESOURCES

The Activist's Handbook: A Primer by Randy Shaw. Berkeley, CA: University of California Press, 2001.

Training for Change (TFC), www.trainingforchange.org TFC offers resources online as well as activist trainings on a range of topics relevant to building strong groups, including setting ground rules, challenging oppression, team-building, meeting and dialogue facilitation, and much more.

Wellstone Action!, www.wellstone.org Wellstone Action! offers training in grassroots activism and running campaigns across the country as well as offering Campus Camp Wellstone, a training conference that students can bring to their own campuses.

04
SPREAD YOUR MESSAGE

COMMUNICATE YOUR PASSION

Think back to how you first became interested in your environmental passions. Did a friend invite you to see a documentary? Did you hear a firsthand account of an environmental travesty from a speakers' tour? Did you read in the newspaper that your favorite park was being turned into condominiums? As we discussed in chapter 1, our activism usually begins by getting educated about an issue. And now that's your job: to speak out green and spread your message.

Spreading your green message can take many forms, from educational forums to film festivals to classroom talks. Yet it all starts with the individual. Whether you are speaking at a rally or are sitting in a classroom when a heated debate erupts, knowing how to communicate powerfully is a crucial way to advance your cause. Take Alec Loorz as an example.

SUCCESS STORY
KIDS VS. GLOBAL WARMING Alec Loorz first saw Al

Gore's documentary *An Inconvenient Truth* when he was twelve years old. Inspired by the message, Alec applied to be a presenter with Gore's The Climate Project, but was turned down due to his age. Undeterred, Alec created his own presentation and gave it more than thirty times to youth and adult audiences in California before Gore took notice.

Eventually Gore invited Alec to his next training session and Alec became the youngest speaker with The Climate Project, giving more than one hundred talks to some twenty thousand people. Later, he founded his own organization, Kids vs. Global Warming, a project of Earth Island Institute, with the mission of educating youth on the science of climate change and empowering them to take action.

Through multimedia presentations to schools, keynote and panel presentations at conferences, videos, and social media, Alec translated the complex science of climate change into terms that motivate youth to get involved with creating solutions.

Alec expressed his bold vision—"to end global warming in my lifetime"—during each and every talk. Of course he knows he can't do it alone, and his ambitious rallying call serves to draw other people to his group.

"Youth have a unique sense of moral authority on this issue.

IT'S OUR PLANET NOW. And we are going to have to

GROW UP AND FACE THE CONSEQUENCES of what

the world does, or fails to do." **—ALEC LOORZ**

© Han Shan

Guess what? Alec didn't start out as a master public speaker. I met him when he was thirteen, and he struck me as a shy teen, though smart and committed. He eventually grew into an enormously captivating speaker through practice. Lots of it. Even if you have glossophobia (fear of public speaking), don't worry—you can beat it.

This chapter will teach you how to be a good storyteller—one of the most important skills you need to be a strong recruiter for your campaign.

Once you've got your messaging down, I'll outline a number of the best methods to spread your message with clarity and passion, from film screenings to classroom presentations and green tours of your community.

STORYTELLING AND PUBLIC SPEAKING

How do you master the art of good communication? It's simple: tell a story, explain your issue, and inspire your audience. Let's start with the basics.

Tell a Story

We loved listening to stories as kids (think: bedtime stories) and we still do. When we hear a good story, the first thing we do is share it with friends and family, right? As in, "Did you hear what happened to Diana?"

We learn from all this storytelling. We learn about the characters in the stories, about how this big crazy world works, and about people doing something memorable, admirable, or diabolical. The most memorable stories stand out from all the background noise. Stories are the fabric we weave to connect with other individuals.

Start telling stories with the story you know best—your own! Have you ever heard the phrase, "People give to people"? It's true! People are often more likely to give money, time, resources, and support to an individual who inspires them rather than to a faceless organization. That's why your personal story is so important. It's an opportunity to share your motivation and your connection to your issue while letting your passion shine through.

So share: how has your life experience prepared you to tackle this issue? Why are you committed to this issue? Often your personal story and motivation are just as important as being an expert on the issue you care about, if not more important. Earth Island Institute ally Ric O'Barry became famous in the 1960s for capturing and training the five dolphins featured in the TV series *Flipper*. When one of the dolphins died, he realized that these amazing creatures weren't destined for captivity, and he devoted his life to freeing captive dolphins. He's such a powerful advocate for the cause precisely because he has a personal connection to the issue.

And then there's my story. In the 1990s, it was discovered that a Unocal oil pipeline—leaking, undetected, for decades—had caused a massive oil spill of hundreds of thousands of gallons underneath Avila Beach, just a dozen miles from my home. The company was forced to clean up the mess, demolishing many of the existing charming buildings and homes in town, digging up and removing the contaminated soil, and changing the entire nature of the beachfront once it was rebuilt. Although it was now cleaner, my beloved Avila Beach had been forever transformed into a tourist-oriented destination, rather than the funky, old-time beach town I'd grown up with.

Being witness to and affected by an oil spill made me a stronger advocate as I continued to speak out against oil contamination and reckless extraction methods in the United States and abroad. Find your personal connection to the story, or the connection of a friend, family member, or neighbor. You will find that people are much more likely to listen to your perspective for a solution on the issue.

Explain Your Issue

Although you don't have to be an expert, you will want to share some concrete information about the issue you're working on. Use real-life stories and examples to complement statistics, facts, and figures. Most people won't remember a bunch of precise statistics and numbers even a few days after hearing you speak, but a powerful mental image can last a lifetime.

What is the most alarming or promising image you can think of, related to your cause? Maybe you're trying to explain the number of people in the community suffering from asthma related to air contamination. Instead of just sharing the statistic, make it visual. Ask everyone who suffers from asthma or respiratory problems to stand. Then invite the rest of the audience members to look for someone they might know or love, standing in that crowd, who's affected. When they return home, they're likely to remember that powerful image of their friends standing in the room—a way of making an issue that once felt distant more real.

Inspire Your Audience

After briefing your audience on the issue and creating mental images designed to stick, your next goal in communication is to inspire and rally other folks to join your efforts. Our generation already understands the severity of our environmental challenges. Focus on what you're going to do to change things, why now is the time for action, and how people can join you in your effort. You want to give people a positive vision to work toward, rather than a negative reality to oppose.

As green jobs leader Van Jones pointed out, Martin Luther King Jr. didn't get famous by saying "I have a complaint." His famous speech, "I have a dream," has endured as one of the most powerful speeches in American history because of its optimistic vision. He didn't spend his whole speech decrying the racism and oppression African-Americans faced, though he certainly spoke to it early in his speech. He spent most of the speech appealing to a vision of a more just America, and he ended his speech by saying that when we let freedom ring "from every village and every hamlet, from every state and every city, we will be able to speed up that day when all of God's children, black men and white men, Jews and Gentiles, Protestants and Catholics, will be able to join hands . . ."

Like King, you can give people a dream to work toward. Although your campus-wide goals may be to set up a food composting program, the bigger dream is moving toward a zero-waste society, right? Show people how your efforts—and theirs, when they step on board—are part of a massive movement for big green changes.

Finally, let people draw their own conclusions from your words. Your audience is intelligent, and they can make their own decisions. If you tell people what to think, you risk alienating them. "You should" or "you need to" language is not nearly as effective as making a compelling argument or sharing a vision to win over their heads and their hearts.

The best public speakers speak from the heart. In what might seem like a contradiction, the best speakers also say the same things, over and over and over again. They don't improvise their speech anew for each event. Van Jones and Lois Gibbs are two of the most compelling, passionate speakers I've seen. Van Jones is a civil rights activist and green jobs advocate; Lois Gibbs fought for the cleanup of Love Canal, a polluted Superfund site in New York. (Superfund sites, by the way, are toxic waste dump sites that the Environmental Protection Agency has prioritized for cleanup.) I have seen both of them speak many times, and their message, stories, and sometimes even entire portions of their speech are consistent, time and again.

When you are speaking in front of others, it can feel like an eternity, as though every moment lasts forever. This isn't a distortion of the space-time continuum; it's just because you're nervous! So remember to take your time and take a deep breath in between sentences. Spend time preparing your talking points—but spend at least as much time practicing the delivery. Don't read your speech word for word; you'll spend more time looking at your notes than at the crowd. Eye contact, connection with the audience, and confidence are more important than getting every word correct.

DEVELOP YOUR ELEVATOR PITCH

So now you've got the main elements of a good speech: your personal story, a compelling description of the issue, and your plans to make big changes. Once your full narrative is polished, you should develop an elevator pitch— a short, powerful overview of your issue and your solution. Why is it called an elevator pitch? Because if a potential supporter were to step into an elevator with you, you would have only about thirty seconds on the way to the chosen floor to get the person engaged in your campaign.

Here's a sample elevator pitch from Dan Rosen. To get off the ground with his new project, Mosaic Ventures, he had to get lots of supporters on board, quickly.

> *I've got unreasonable news for you. Our project, Mosaic Ventures, is one step away from being selected into the Unreasonable Institute! If Mosaic is selected, I will be spending ten weeks based out of Boulder, Colorado, and will be using the time to build our team, create a razor-sharp business plan, align with strategic partners, and give this venture wings as it takes flight.*

> *The idea of Mosaic Ventures is to form a renewable energy investment fund financed by Native American and outside capital to make investments into the emerging cleantech market. Reservations are ideal sites for scale-up of cleantech innovations. If Native American tribes play a major role in the decarbonization of the U.S. economy, it will mean sustainable prosperity for tribes and regions (turning rust belts into green belts), the creation of gigawatts of renewable energy, and taking a stab at climate change, polluting fossil fuels, and dependency on oil.*

> *The finalists were chosen from over forty-five countries and now enter into what is called the "Finalist Marketplace." The first twenty-five*

fellows who raise $6,500 get a place at the Institute. My goal is to get out of the gate running and get 650 people to donate.

I would be grateful if you would vote for me with your dollars and send out a request to your friends, families, and networks asking them to do the same. Can I count on you to be one of my first supporters?

You will use your elevator pitch time and again: to recruit fellow volunteers, to inspire people to give resources and financial support, and to quickly and effectively tell the media about your work. It helps to finish your pitch with a clear and easy hook so that if someone is interested in your campaign they can follow up. As in Dan's pitch, usually this hook involves a yes or no question ("Can I count on you to be one of my supporters?"). Practice your pitch out loud and get feedback from friends until it is compelling, concise, and clear.

EVENTS TO SPREAD YOUR MESSAGE

Now that you've polished your own communication skills, it's time to put together some cool events that give you a chance to talk about your cause. Public forums advance critical thinking and provide a space for dialogue, action, and publicity for pressing environmental issues. Film screenings, classroom outreach, toxic and green tours, workshops, theater performances, teach-ins, and speaker events all provide an opportunity to grow the number of individuals united for social change.

No matter what event you're hosting, a great way to welcome guests is to set up an informational table at the entrance of the room or outdoor space. Greet guests, capture their contact details, and give them some literature and tools to work on the issue after the event is over.

In addition, partner with other student groups or community organizations to cosponsor your event and promote it to their networks. If you are a student, look to the campus newspaper, radio station, or TV station, to see whether they'll do a pitch for the event as well. Ask professors or teachers to offer extra credit to their students who attend and to make an announcement in their class about the event. Forward email invitations to your friends, faculty, staff, and campus offices like the residence halls.

EVENT GREENING TIPS

If you're going to organize an event to raise environmental consciousness, then it only makes sense to "walk the talk" by greening the event itself. Here are a few tips:

Offering food? You should: it's a great draw, especially for the under-twenty-five crowd. Serve local, seasonal, and organic fare whenever possible and offer options for vegetarians and vegans. When buying food and other supplies, choose items with little packaging, or buy in bulk. Use washable dishware or biodegradable dishware made from cornstarch or sugar cane. If you are going to use disposable dishware, make sure it's compostable, like nonwaxy paper plates without plastic lining. Avoid Styrofoam and petroleum products like plastic cups. Encourage folks to bring their own mugs; offer water stations rather than water bottles.

For print materials at the event and for publicity posters and flyers, try to use 100-percent PCW, PCF paper (post-consumer waste, processed chlorine-free). If you use a printing house to make posters, ask whether they can use soy-based inks. If you use plastic name badges at the event, reuse them. Set up a clearly labeled recycling area (composting too, if you offer it), and if recycling or composting isn't common practice in your community, have a volunteer assigned to the trash area to encourage people to recycle appropriate materials.

Encourage carpooling, cycling, and walking to and from the event, and promote public transportation options. Tell people about these eco-friendly arrangements on all of your outreach materials.

To do community outreach, hang posters, chalk sidewalks, promote the event in your community newspaper's online and print calendars, leave flyers in key locations, send email invites and text messages to friends and family, and use social networking tools like Facebook and MySpace to create event invitations or post updates to your personal profile page. You can even use the media to recruit attendees and also to cover your issue. (See chapter 8, Make Media Headlines, for more strategies for working with the media.)

Each and every one of the strategies I describe can help build the green movement in your community; which one you choose depends on what most excites you and your fellow group members.

EVENT ATTENDANCE

Be specific about how many people you want at your event. A "big" audience means different things to different people. You might think a big audience is twenty-five students, whereas your friend thinks it's a group of two hundred. So be clear, specific, and practical in your numerical goals. Once you've got a target number for recruitment, you can craft an appropriate outreach strategy using the advertising tactics discussed in chapter 3, Build a Green Movement. And remember the law of halves from the last chapter: on average, only half of the people who sign up to attend an event will actually show up.

Film Screenings

Did watching *An Inconvenient Truth* move you to take action, the way it did for Alec Loorz of Kids vs. Global Warming? Consider hosting a movie screening of your favorite documentary film. Movies can rally individuals and spark hope, outrage, or inspiration in ways that books, articles, and lectures might not.

Here's how to make it happen:

STEP 1: GET THE FILM.

For public screenings, you'll need to confirm that your film has been licensed for public viewings. You can buy educational and documentary films for this purpose through companies like The Video Project, borrow films from groups like Campus Progress that have purchased films for this very purpose, or check in with your school's administration or film department about their film library.

STEP 2: FIGURE OUT THE LOGISTICS.

Estimate the number of individuals you think will attend. Are you talking 15 or 150? If the room is too big for the number of attendees, it will feel cavernous and empty. If it's too small, people will have to stand along the walls or be turned away. Like Goldilocks, you're looking for the perfect fit. Get a theater or a room with some slight slope or elevation to the rows of chairs, so people sitting in the back can see as well as those in the front. To screen films in a room with no slope, stagger the rows of chairs to provide sight lines. Are folks likely to come during the lunch hour? In the afternoon? Evening? Select the date and time when you think you'll draw the largest crowd and reserve the room.

STEP 3: TEST THE TECH SYSTEM.
At least a week before the event, make sure your tech system is in good working order. Will you be using a projector and a screen or a large television? Find a tech support person to be on hand in advance of the event and through the end of the film.

STEP 4: SPREAD THE WORD.
How does Hollywood recruit moviegoers? Advertising! You should do the same using the outreach ideas mentioned earlier in this chapter.

STEP 5: HOST AN INSPIRING EVENT.
Set up the room in advance, including some information tables. You can place materials for people to take home on or under each chair. Remember, people are there to watch the films, so limit the talking. Thank folks for coming, introduce your group and its key members, talk very briefly about the film, then let it roll.

STEP 6: MOBILIZE THE CROWD.
After the film, people will be fired up to take action, though they will also probably be antsy to get out of their chairs and go home. Don't keep the entire audience captive in their chairs for long talks! Instead, offer a way for people to take action quickly when they're still excited about the issue. Ask them to write a letter to a member of congress (make it easy by putting blank paper under each chair before the event starts), make a phone call, sign up for your next campaign meeting, or take some other immediate next step. If you want to follow up with more conversation after the film, break into small groups or invite people to stay on for a quick overview of how they can get more involved.

Classroom Outreach

Young kids can be some of the most powerful ambassadors for environmental sustainability. That said, lots of educators don't have the knowledge to incorporate environmental literacy and teaching into their classrooms.

Take your eco-message into the classroom of local elementary schools. You can help build kids' understanding of and commitment to sustainability, and maybe the teacher's, too!

STEP 1: FIND OR DRAFT YOUR LESSON PLAN.

Have a clear outline of your lesson plan to share with the teacher, including your goals and topics, the length of time needed to deliver your lesson, and interactive activities for the students. Facing the Future (www .facingthefuture.org) and Earth Day Network (www.earthday.org) are two organizations that provide free downloadable curriculum and sample lessons plans online, if you'd prefer not to draft your own.

STEP 2: FIND A SCHOOL AND TEACHER.

Find the appropriate grade for your lesson plan, then approach teachers at that school with a phone call and email requesting the opportunity to work in their classroom. Be clear about your goals: is this a one-time visit, or are you committed to repeat visits? Why are you interested in working in their school? What experience, if any, do you have in delivering this lesson plan and working with kids?

STEP 3: PRACTICE YOUR DELIVERY.

You want to be a hit on your first trip to the school. The best way to do this is advance practice. Run through your entire lesson plan at least twice with an audience (including handing out materials, showing films, or setting up any displays you need). Younger siblings make great test audiences. If they're confused or bored, that will help you improve your delivery. Practice giving instructions and moderating the interactive exercises; see whether the exercises take the amount of time you expect and generate the results you want.

STEP 4: WOW THE KIDS.

On the day of your visit, introduce yourself in a fun and accessible way before you get started with the lesson. Connect with the kids by getting them talking in the first five minutes of your visit. Ask questions, solicit lots of answers, and show a real interest in what the kids have to say. Then it's your turn: dive into the lesson plan.

STEP 5: DEBRIEF YOUR VISIT.

After the class, ask the teacher for honest and constructive feedback. Don't worry if you didn't get everything just right—that's to be expected. They teach every day; you don't! Feedback will help improve your teaching for future visits.

Zander Srodes, a young student himself, used classroom visits to help build support for the protection of sea turtles in Florida, which led to his next adventure: creating educational materials that could be used worldwide!

SUCCESS STORY

TURTLE TALKS Walking the beaches of southwest Florida, sixth-grader **Zander Srodes** saw yellow stakes in the sand that notified beach-goers of the nests of loggerhead and green turtles, both species at risk of extinction due to commercial fisheries and habitat destruction. Each year volunteers patrolled the beach and kept statistics on the success or failure of every nest on the coast of Florida. When Zander started walking the beach he became aware of the dismal future of these animals. That summer, when he was just eleven years old, he had a dream of creating his own educational program to inform kids and adults about how they could help the fate of these ancient and charismatic reptiles.

Zander heard that a local foundation was offering grants to youth. He applied for funding, then made an appointment to meet with sea turtle biologists at a nearby marine lab to gather slides and materials to share. Equipped with knowledge, a slide projector, and a homemade sea turtle costume, Zander asked local educators whether he could teach their students. He was welcomed into numerous schools, and his marine science road show rapidly became a hit along the Gulf Coast.

Still, one-time visits and assemblies weren't enough. Zander wanted to create age-appropriate printed material for his audience. He wasn't able to find existing materials, so he wrote his own children's activity book. The book has been translated into four languages and given away free to more than one hundred thousand kids and adults worldwide.

"While sea turtles are my main focus, my teachings are relevant to other species. If you are **PROTECTING SEA TURTLES** you are protecting a lot of other creatures in the environment." **—ZANDER SRODES**

Zander didn't start out with the intention of printing a book that would be used worldwide—he just wanted to educate local school kids—but he touched upon a huge need. With kids ages six through eleven spending twenty-eight hours a week in front of the television (according to the Nielsen company) and very little time outdoors, you may just be their only link to hearing more about the environment, whether you're talking about local issues or worldwide concerns.

Green Tours and Toxic Tours

Explore your community or neighborhood inside and out. Gather a group of friends, start walking, and take note of your community's environmental assets—positive things like green buildings, clean energy production sites, organic gardens, and environmentally friendly businesses. In addition, document the negatives—polluting power plants, refineries, chemical sites, Superfund sites, and brownfields (abandoned and under-used industrial or commercial properties). This is a great start to finding out what resources are available to the community and what things may need some improvement.

Once you know what you have to work with, organize a tour to educate members of your community. Your tours might focus on your community's assets (a Green Tour) or the hazards (a Toxic Tour). Green tours help green innovators pass the torch to a new generation of change-makers and can cover a number of areas:

> ➤ Business: Tours feature sustainable businesses, focusing on companies that provide environmentally sound goods and services. This tour can inspire other business owners to adopt energy-efficient and low-waste practices.

> ➤ Energy: Tours feature electric and biodiesel cars, alternative fueling stations, and alternative energy production such as solar and wind,

showing community members how they can shift their consumption to cleaner forms of energy.

➤ Agriculture: Tours visit community and organic gardens, farmers markets, and sustainable restaurants. A green tour of community gardens, for example, may introduce local residents to opportunities to create their own plot at home or at the garden.

➤ Green building: Tours spotlight green architecture, green building certification systems, and resource-efficient design. A tour of green homes can show people how to save on their energy and water bills by adopting green practices and newer technologies; a green dorm room tour can build a buzz about sustainability on campus.

Toxic tours, in contrast, spotlight little-known environmental hazards. Toxic tours not only educate the public but can also spur decision making. The media scrutiny and public attention you draw could motivate city and industry officials to clean up their act. For example, you might time the tour to coincide with local elections or votes on budgets relating to city funds for cleanups.

Creating a tour can require months of planning to set up the tour stops, recruit participants, and do media outreach. Is your group capable of investing this time, and is this the best use of your energy? If so, here's how to get started.

STEP 1: EXPLORE YOUR COMMUNITY.

Take inventory of the assets and toxics. Do some research on green sites as well as toxic sites. If you discover a potentially toxic site, research which chemicals are emitted and any environmental and health threats. This can be done through tools such as the Environmental Protection Agency's Toxic Release Inventory (www.epa.gov/TRI).

STEP 2: BRAINSTORM YOUR STOPS.

Are you clear on the audience that will best benefit from this tour? For example, you should design a very different tour for small-business owners looking for inspiration from business colleagues than for students exploring green careers.

Get clear on your tour goal and audience, then dream up a list of every possible tour stop for your issue focus with a map in hand. Walking tours are best—keep the stops within walking distance for a 90- to 120-minute tour. If stops are spread out, you'll have to arrange for transportation, which can be costly and logistically challenging.

STEP 3: DETERMINE GOALS FOR EACH STOP.

What are the key educational messages to share at this stop? How long will the group need to stay at the site? Who will they need to talk to? Will you need to set up interviews with staff or volunteers at the site?

Tailor your facts to the age range of your audience. For example, in a toxic tour, you won't need to get into much depth about chemical pollutants for elementary school children, but with adults and college students you may want to get as in-depth as possible. Create trivia questions to make the tour more interactive as you walk through the neighborhood.

STEP 4: GET PERMISSION.

Connect with the business or property owners at each of the sites. If you are doing stops outside of a business or property (or are spotlighting toxic sites), you will not need permission, but if you would like to do interviews with the staff or tour the premises, get permission for a stop. Clearly delineate what the site visit will entail and how long it will last.

STEP 5: DO A RUN-THROUGH OF THE TOUR.

For your first few tours, select at least three individuals to staff the tour; one to act as tour guide and emcee, another to liaise with the site staff and volunteers during each stop (and assist tour participants with any questions), and one to liaise with the press. Take a group of your peers on a run-through of the tour and see how long the tour actually takes; groups can move slowly between sites! Work out any kinks before the actual debut of the tour. Eventually, with more familiarity, one person can lead an entire tour alone.

STEP 6: ADVERTISE FOR THE TOUR(S).

Once you've got a solid tour planned, set a day and time (or multiple tour dates) and begin advertising to the public. Although it can be challenging to recruit public officials to participate in the tour, try! If your goal is to influence public officials, and they refuse to attend your toxic tour, invite "secondary" targets—individuals who have an influence over your target. For toxic tours, for example, this could include doctors, nurses, and public health figures, who may later turn out to be strong allies in your cleanup campaign.

STEP 7: INVITE THE MEDIA.

Of course you'll have to convince reporters that you have a newsworthy and fresh story here. If you're successful, the resulting story could put pressure on your target to take action.

STEP 8: WANT TO TAKE IT A STEP FURTHER?

With a camera or video camera, document all the stops on your tour. Then create a Google map to pinpoint your tour sites. Once you do this, you can upload images, videos, statistics, and descriptions relevant to each site on to your Google map. This creates an interactive multimedia tour that can be seen by anyone globally. Marisol Becerra did this in Chicago, Illinois, to share her community's story with the wider world.

SUCCESS STORY
THE CLOUD FACTORY Marisol Becerra was a freshman in

high school in Chicago, Illinois, when she went on a toxic tour led by a local nonprofit group called the Little Village Environmental Justice Organization (LVEJO). From LVEJO, she learned that the Harvard School of Public Health had determined that the health problems and asthma that so many of her family members and neighbors experienced were directly linked to the two coal-burning power plants within blocks of her house.

When she was young, she called the power plant nearest her house "The Cloud Factory," due to the gigantic gray clouds it released. On this tour, she learned the coal plant released dangerous chemicals, like nitrous oxide and sulfur dioxide. These chemicals were responsible for 41 premature deaths, 500 emergency room visits, and 2,500 asthma attacks per year.

Marisol began volunteering with LVEJO to conduct an extensive mapping of the toxics and assets in Little Village. After inventorying 150 blocks, she decided to organize a youth group that could use technology to raise

awareness and mobilize others to join a national campaign for environmental justice. She began leading Community Assets and Toxics tours and
taught other youth to do the same, with more than fifteen youth ultimately
leading tours. After hosting several workshops on media technologies as
tools for community organizing, these young people began making films
about their community. They posted data about local industrial polluters
on an interactive Google map, embedded with personal stories, statistics,
photographs, and videos.

Marisol's youth group soon became one of the most active youth
environmental justice groups nationally, speaking at over fifty meetings,
conferences, and events in front of thousands of people.

"Our map **RAISED AWARENESS LOCALLY AND
NATIONALLY** about the extent of the environmental
injustice and health problems that my community suffers
each and every day, **WHERE WE LIVE, WORK,
AND PLAY.**" —**MARISOL BECCERA**

Speaker Series and Debates

Hosting a speaker or a debate series can spark thoughtful conversation
about your issue. If you are a student and your campus already offers a
speaker or lecture program, go through those channels to find funding and
an infrastructure to support the process. Consider modifying the event into
an assembly for the entire student body, where you have a captive audience
of your peers for a half hour or more!

STEP 1: SET YOUR GOALS AND BRAINSTORM POTENTIAL SPEAKERS.

Are you looking to educate folks, stir up controversy and open up dialogue, or inspire people to take action? For a lively debate, invite folks
from both ends of the political spectrum; to move your campaign forward and inspire action, invite only advocates for your cause. Nonlocal
speakers often request an honorarium and/or travel fees—if you have
no budget, see whether a local campus will pay the fees. Otherwise,

invite local academics, professionals, student activists, authors, or media figures to speak.

Aim high and get the most famous individual on the topic that you can with the resources you have available. If you are targeting faculty, invite popular professors; consider inviting the chair of your campus sustainability committee. Not everyone will say yes, so choose some alternative speakers to ask. Ensure diversity of panel members, in terms of age, ethnicity, gender, class, or any other criteria you think are important. Diverse panels attract diverse audiences.

STEP 2: LOGISTICS.

Find a date, time, and location for the event. You can host the event on any educational campus or at a local library or community center. Early evening events, Monday through Thursday, typically draw the largest crowds; weekend events are often flops. Avoid times and dates that conflict with other events happening in the school, local community, or town. For example, if sports are big in your town, don't schedule an event to conflict with major sporting events, like Monday night football. If you're inviting a big-name speaker, you'll want to be flexible to find a date that works for the speaker's schedule.

STEP 3: GET A COMMITMENT.

Invite your speakers: three to four panel members is ideal. Reach out with an invitation up to three times, via phone, email, and mail; if you don't hear back after the third approach, the person is probably not interested. Confirm your speakers at least one month in advance of your event so you can begin advertising. Help panelists prepare by giving them parameters for the night, including the event's goals and expected attendees and demographic of the audience, and outlining the event's structure, including the amount of time they will have to speak. Five to ten minutes per person is ideal for multiple panelists; allow twenty minutes for a solo speaker. Panelists will often speak for longer than you ask them to—so if you ask them to prepare a five-minute speech, they may well talk for ten. Factor that into your timing.

STEP 4: TREAT YOUR SPEAKERS LIKE GOLD.
Call them a week in advance to confirm the event details and their participation. If they are out-of-towners, pick them up and drop them off from the airport, train, or bus station, escort them to their lodging, and orient them on campus. Escorting out-of-town speakers to the event is the best way to ensure they arrive on time and don't get lost. Ask all speakers to arrive thirty to forty-five minutes early for an orientation; you can entice them by providing food on site.

STEP 5: RUN A GREAT EVENT.
Select a panel moderator who can keep time, introduce the panelists and the night's theme, and thank the event sponsors. After speeches, open up the conversation for questions and answers from the audience. The moderator can invite people to fill out note cards with their questions and select among those, invite people to queue up at a microphone to ask questions, or call for the audience members to raise their hands. Limit the introduction, speakers, and Q & A to an hour or less and reserve the rest of the time at the event for informal socializing.

NEXT STOP: POLITICS

Education is just the start. Don't stop there! If the whole world is educated but not taking action to bring about needed changes, we'll be left with an educated public and a devastated planet.

Education provides the platform to grow your supporters and get people more engaged. The next chapter will show you how to turn commitment into action by passing laws and influencing officials (or stepping into office yourself!).

RESOURCES

Campus Progress, www.campusprogress.org Campus Progress works to help young people—advocates, activists, journalists, artists, and others—make their voices heard on issues that matter. They connect young people with the speakers, films, grants, and resources needed to set up engaging panels, film screenings, spoken word performances, rallies, and more.

Facing the Future, www.facingthefuture.org Facing the Future offers free K-12 lesson plans in sustainability and global issues.

Speak Out, www.speakoutnow.org Speak Out organizes workshops, trainings, and educational institutes to strengthen social justice organizing at high schools, colleges, and universities, and in communities nationwide.

The Video Project, www.videoproject.com The Video Project distributes environmental videos about the fate of the planet, including Oscar and Emmy award-winners from over two hundred independent filmmakers worldwide.

Youth Speaks, www.youthspeaks.org Youth Speaks is the leading nonprofit presenter of spoken word performance, education, and youth development programs in the country. If you want to learn how to incorporate spoken word and writing into your movement for environmental change, this is the place to start.

05
POLITICS

HOW TO LOBBY POLITICIANS, PASS LEGISLATION, AND RUN FOR OFFICE

How can you use your voice and influence as a young person to get the government to respond to your issues? Stake out a place in the political process to influence the way policy is made. If you are over eighteen, voting is a great start, but there are many ways for people of all ages to influence public policy, which includes the laws, plans, funding priorities, and actions of our government.

Getting involved in shaping public policy ensures that the voices and issues that are marginalized have an opportunity to be pushed to the center of public debate—where they belong! Plus, policy drives investment in crucial public infrastructure and sets our nation's priorities. For example, policy at many levels of government, from local to national, helps determine the energy sources we use, where and how our food is grown, the availability of public transportation options, and the land we protect and develop.

This chapter will introduce you to different ways to get involved in the political process, from passing resolutions to registering and turning out more young voters for critical elections, and finally, stepping into office yourself. You can also lobby for (or against) proposed legislation, as Alex Lin did, before he was even old enough to vote.

SUCCESS STORY
SO EASY EVEN KIDS CAN DO IT When Alex Lin was

just eleven years old, he heard in the news about the growing e-waste crisis. E-waste refers to electronic equipment—like computers—bound for the waste stream. This equipment often contains toxic heavy metals such as lead, cadmium, and mercury. If disposed of improperly, these metals can cause serious human health problems like permanent brain damage, cancer, and damage to the nervous and immune systems.

So Alex joined with his friends to hold a recycling drive to collect the buildup of e-waste in his small hometown of Westerly, Rhode Island. They contacted the manager of a local recycling company. Because the company stood to gain revenue from breaking down and selling the electronics, the company was happy to send an eighteen-wheeler truck to pick up the electronics that the recycling drive brought in. In a single day, the team collected two full truckloads of e-waste.

But Alex knew that a one-day e-waste drive wasn't enough to solve the problem. His team needed to come up with an efficient way to keep a recycling container available to the community at all times. So Alex set up a partnership with the same recycling company, which installed a permanent receptacle for e-waste and collected more than three hundred thousand pounds of e-waste in the first few years, equal to the weight of about seventy-five SUVs.

After persuading his school superintendent to make refurbishing donated computers part of his school's computer curriculum, Alex and his team worked with the computer classes to reclaim and rebuild computers donated by students and their families. The school restored and distributed over three hundred computers, and Alex's team set up computer centers in Rhode Island, Mexico, Kenya, Cameroon, Sri Lanka, and the Philippines.

"Is it enough?" Alex wondered. His group decided it wasn't. As the next step in the campaign, the group started working with legislators on proposed e-waste legislation for the state of Rhode Island. The bill had been in the works for four years, and each year it had failed to pass. Alex and his team reevaluated the bill's positive and negative points and came to the conclusion that the bill was too complicated.

Alex drafted a sample resolution to ban the dumping of e-waste and worked with city officials in Westerly to adopt the resolution. Those officials sent their resolution to the state legislators, who revised their own bill based on its language. The team spent an entire spring lobbying; they got petitions signed, made presentations to community groups, and testified several times at the Rhode Island State House. Finally, victory! In July 2006, Rhode Island became the fourth state in the nation to adopt a bill requiring proper disposal of electronic waste.

"One of our greatest strengths when working with legislation was a working model. So we could go to the state and say, 'Hey. **THIS WORKS.** It's so easy **EVEN KIDS CAN DO IT**.'" —ALEX LIN

© Drew Altizer

Alex was only eleven when he began his project and thirteen when the legislation was passed. Pretty impressive, no? As you can see from Alex's story, a small handful of youth activists with the right allies have the power to shape laws. You can make it easier for people to do the right thing than to do the wrong thing. For example, imagine the uproar if people were allowed to buy electronics only one day out of the year. In some places, you can recycle electronics only one day out of the year. We need to make it just as easy for people to recycle toxic products as it is for them to buy them. Laws and public policy are one of the best strategies for changing the status quo.

LOBBYING

Lobbying, or the practice of influencing government policy, can take many forms—from phone calls, letters, emails, and visits to policy makers, to speaking at public hearings and events. Lobbying may seem intimidating at first, but it's actually remarkably easy. Public officials are often incredibly eager to hear the perspectives of young people.

First, it's best to link up with advocacy groups and local nonprofits that work on your issue. They might agree to lobby with you or steer you to other resources and contacts, and they will know about any pending legislation that needs to be supported or opposed. With their help, identify your decision-makers. As you'll remember from chapter 2, Create an Action Plan, a decision-maker is a specific individual with the power to make a decision about your issue, such as a particular legislator, rather than an entire body of individuals, like Congress.

If you want to learn more about the legislative process, Project Vote Smart (www.projectvotesmart.org) is a great resource. You can also learn more about the process by having meetings with local legislators: Alex discovered that the bill's sponsoring legislators were more than happy to get together for strategy and coaching meetings. It can also be really beneficial to make friends with the legislator's staffers. Staffers are the gatekeepers to the legislators and often help translate the language and demands from community advocates into the bill's language. However, you don't have to know the ins and outs of lawmaking to be a strong lobbyist for your cause.

When selecting a decision-maker to lobby, realize that you don't need to reach everyone. In terms of legislation, you can group officials into supporters, the opposition, and the undecideds. Let's say you're working for the passage of federal climate change legislation. The supporters are individuals who have already committed to vote yes on the bill or those that have cosigned onto the bill as supporters. The opposition has publicly declared their intention to vote no on the bill. You won't focus on these groups—they have already made up their minds. Instead, focus on the undecideds—officials who may lean toward your perspective but haven't publicly declared a position. Your goal is to turn the "I might support the bill" folks into "I'm definitely supporting the bill."

Once you identify your decision-makers, you have to decide how to reach out to them. Call-ins, letter-writing campaigns, and email blasts typically work best in two cases: when you can't meet face-to-face and when there's a time-sensitive decision coming up, like a vote or a final ruling on a court case. However, if you have the opportunity to appear live and in person at meetings, public hearings, or public events, take advantage of that opportunity to leave a lasting impression with your decision-makers.

Often a combination of outreach techniques are needed. Amir Nadav and his team collected petitions, reached out to allies at the state capitol through lobby meetings, and hosted a rally on the state capitol steps as part of a series of tactics designed to protect students from diesel fumes. Read on to find out how he won his School Bus Diesel Campaign, in record time!

SUCCESS STORY
THE SCHOOL BUS DIESEL CAMPAIGN In his junior

year in high school, **Amir Nadav** attended a planning meeting of the Sierra Club's Air Toxics Committee. That night, a variety of issues were discussed, including studies about the health effects of diesel exhaust. Amir learned that diesel exhaust spewed by school buses in Minnesota contained forty known toxic chemicals and fifteen carcinogens, and that federal regulators estimated that diesel exhaust is responsible for 125,000 cases of cancer nationwide. He also learned that diesel fumes can aggravate asthma and allergies and are a major source of particulate pollution, which causes 70,000 deaths in the United States each year.

In Minnesota, asthma was the leading cause of school absenteeism. Amir teamed up with his high school friends and the North Star Chapter of the Sierra Club to create the School Bus Diesel Campaign. The students created posters to put up in their schools and drafted a petition. They approached teachers and asked for a few minutes to speak before each class. After giving a two-minute talk about the issue and what they thought students could do, they invited everyone to sign the petition. Their campaign goal was to deliver five hundred signatures to someone in power.

After Air Toxics Coordinator Paula Maccabee took the issue to a number of the Sierra Club's allies at the Minnesota state capitol, passing a state law became a viable idea. From that point on everything happened quickly. The students had started the petition in January and by mid-February a Senate committee agreed to hold a hearing on a proposed bill that would address their concerns. It was important for students to be visibly involved in lobbying for the cause, so four students testified in support of the law to protect their health.

The student leaders and the local Sierra Club chapter thought that a strong show of support might influence Minnesota lawmakers, so they decided to host a rally on the steps of the state capitol. They approached sympathetic teachers with the idea and got them to agree to host a field trip for the rally. The night before, the students made dozens of signs for the rally. The day of the rally was sunny with blue skies. Buses pulled up at the capitol steps in Saint Paul and 150 students poured out to chant and march in a circle on the steps for half an hour. Following speeches by students, advocates, and lawmakers, the students presented their signed petitions to the Senate majority leader.

The bill passed the Minnesota State Senate in the final weeks of the legislative session in 2002, and the governor signed it into law just days later. The bill's supporters were able to use youth involvement as leverage at the eleventh hour to get the legislation passed, citing all the students relying on them to pass this legislation.

"I didn't think I could make much of a difference. Yet by **MOBILIZING HIGH SCHOOL STUDENTS** and teaming up with local advocacy groups, **WE HELPED BUILD A STRONG, UNITED VOICE** that could not be ignored."
—AMIR NADAV

Like Amir, you can convince everyone you know (and even strangers who agree with you!) to sign petitions, call, email, or write letters to the people whose opinions you are trying to sway.

Phone Calls, Letter-Writing Pushes, and Email Blasts

These forms of communication are best for time-sensitive issues. For example, if your elected official has not yet announced his or her support for strong climate change legislation coming up for a vote in less than a month, encourage the official to vote yes. If you're writing with more advance notice, take it a step further and ask him or her to cosponsor the bill.

Typically, letters and phone calls carry the most weight, whereas emails, because they're easier to dash off, aren't given quite as much consideration (though they still help). Petitions are important, but if people are just signing their name on a list it's not as powerful as sharing their opinion in their own words.

Elected officials and their staff generally assume that for every individual who makes a call or writes a letter, another one hundred individuals feel the same way but haven't taken the time to say so. That means each call you make or letter you send represents one hundred calls or letters to your target. Wow! See how your outreach can really make a difference?

Here's some guidance for coordinating a massive push, particularly just before a time-sensitive vote.

STEP 1: CHOOSE YOUR TACTIC.

Choose your form of communication: phone, email, or letters. A call-in day is a concentrated one-day push to generate a flood of calls to your target. In this case, using cell phones is best, because you can travel on foot to where potential supporters are. If you're asking people to write letters (or sign preprinted postcards with a message to your target), you'll need to provide pens, paper, and clipboards. If you're doing an email push, you can either rely on spreading the word digitally or gather some portable laptops with internet access, so people can stop at that very moment to log into their email account and take action. Start by gathering the supplies you'll need. At this stage, look for partner organizations with large memberships and outreach "muscle" to blast their membership about your big push.

STEP 2: ADVERTISE WHEN AND WHERE.

Plan to set up shop where the bulk of your supporters can be found. On campus, this could be outside of the library, cafeteria, or gym; in your community, hit up coffee shops, movie theaters, malls, or any other places where people congregate. If you're hosting the event on campus, start doing outreach and education to your peers. Ask your teachers for permission to make a short announcement in class and then collect letters there. Use signs, banners, and visuals to pique the interest of fellow students on the big day. Use the same advertising tactics you used to build your group (see page 35). For community efforts, simply show up with a big volunteer crew, amplified with posters and visuals that draw attention to your group and explain what you're doing. Make sure you're hosting the event on public property or have asked for permission to be in front of businesses.

STEP 3: DRAFT A SCRIPT OR SAMPLE TEXT.

For emails and letters, draft sample text that people can copy: three paragraphs max for emails and no more than one page for letters. Make your concerns and your request clear. What do you want the policy maker to do? Allocate funds for an environmental cleanup? Vote for a piece of legislation? Sign on in support of your campaign? If you're lobbying about a specific bill, identify its number and title.

When writing, include your contact details so policy makers can follow up via email or mail to share what they've done on your issue. For phone calls, give your peers a phone script so they know what to say. In each case, make sure your supporters identify their relationship to the target, particularly if they live in an area the target represents.

STEP 4: HOLD THE TARGET ACCOUNTABLE.

Finally, design a form to record the total number of calls, emails, or letters generated. If you are doing a massive call-in, also record what response you received, because your target (or a representative) will respond immediately. If you are sending letters, postcards, and emails, you will typically receive a response within a few days to a week. Use this information to reach out to the media with a story, like "250 Students Call on Congressman Perkins to Take Action," which can generate even more pressure on your target. See chapter 8, Make Media Headlines, for more suggestions on pitching stories to the media.

If your targeted official later fails to take action as promised, send a reminder to him or her on behalf of your team. Here's an example: "Dear Congressman Perkins: Remember last month when you responded to ·our phone call-in, saying you would sign on as a cosponsor for clean air legislation in our state by March 1st? It's mid-March, and you still have not cosigned the bill. The 250 students who called you are watching to make sure you fulfill your promise. It's time for action."

Robin Bryan employed a letter-writing campaign to demonstrate widespread support for the protection of the boreal forest in Canada—and ended up convincing legislators to save nearly a million acres of forest!

SUCCESS STORY
DREAM BIG, ACT FAST, AND LEAD BY EXAMPLE

EXAMPLE **Robin Bryan**, twenty-one, used a letter drive as a tactic in a campaign to protect nearly one million acres of boreal forest in Manitoba, Canada—the world's largest single land storehouse of carbon and its most abundant source of fresh water. While completing his degree at the University of Winnipeg, Robin led the campaign against logging in Manitoba's provincial parks. He organized rallies, spoke with elected officials, delivered classroom presentations about the issue, and fundraised tirelessly. Robin also set out to collect ten thousand letters to the provincial government, calling for protection of the East Shore Wilderness Area. Through spending hundreds of his own hours going door-to-door in his community and by mobilizing volunteers on campus and from nearby high school environmental groups, Robin met his goal. These letters, and the awareness they raised, were key to the campaign victory. In 2008, Robin was rewarded for his efforts when the Manitoba government banned logging in four of the five parks with logging operations, setting nearly a million acres off-limits to industrial logging.

© Han Shan

"If I didn't begin to **DREAM BIG, ACT FAST, AND LEAD BY EXAMPLE**, I felt that I would have to sit back and watch a historic opportunity pass me by." **—ROBIN BRYAN**

The letter drive was crucial to Robin's success. In fact, after gathering public comments the next logical step is delivering them to the policy maker—ideally in person.

Visits to Policy Makers

You'll find that policy makers are usually eager to meet with young con-stituents. It's generally easier to meet with elected officials at the state or federal level when the legislature is not in session. If you want to pass a law at the state or federal level, open a line of communication with your elected officials early on—especially if you want them to write and introduce a bill.

There are four main steps to having a successful meeting with a policy maker: scheduling the meeting, preparing for it, executing it, and follow-ing up.

STEP 1: SCHEDULE THE MEETING.

To find elected representatives in your district, visit www.congress .org/congressorg/dbq/officials or www.usa.gov/Contact/Elected.shtml. For representatives and senators in the federal and state capitols, call the legislative assistant or another staff member. In the case of local officials, you may be able to reach them directly; if not, speak to their assistants. Be persistent—sometimes it takes a few follow-up calls or letters to con-firm a meeting. Sometimes officials will need to send a staff person in their place; treat their staff member with the same courtesy and respect you would give the official.

STEP 2: PREPARE FOR THE MEETING.

Small meetings of five people or fewer are ideal; with a smaller contin-gent you won't overwhelm their staff, at least for a first meeting. In the future, if you want to demonstrate widespread support for the issue, you can schedule follow-up meetings with larger groups.

Research your official's current stance and past voting record (if appli-cable) on the issue. Be organized: know your goals, roles, and agenda going into the meeting. Although you may be passionate about many issues, stick to one or two key issues per meeting. Plan roles for everyone attending, and do practice run-throughs of the meeting in advance, at least twice, to ensure that your team will be prepared, organized, and articulate.

STEP 3: EXECUTE A GREAT MEETING.

On the big day, dress professionally—try to match the appearance and manner of those you expect to meet in the office—and arrive early. If you do happen to be running late, call to give advance notice.

Start the meeting with introductions, and tell the policy maker why he or she should listen to you—if you have a personal story or connection to your issue, share that. Deliver letters from citizens in your district, a signed petition from your fellow students, drawings and notes from elementary school kids, or some other form of "care package" that helps educate the official about constituents' views.

Politely direct the conversation—remember your goals and your agenda—even when the politician or staffer veers off-course. Answer their questions; if you don't know the answer, say, "I don't know." Certainly offer to get back to them with the answer later, but make the offer only if you are sure you will remember to follow up.

The most important part of the entire meeting will be your request for support. Make a clear ask—"Where do you stand on the proposed clean energy legislation, and how will you vote?"—and listen for the response. If the policy maker doesn't give you a clear answer, state that you are still unclear on his or her position, and ask again. You can ask the policy maker to sign onto a bill as a cosponsor, to vote for or against proposed legislation, or to speak about the issue at your school, at an upcoming protest, or at a community forum. You should offer help, as well; ask the official how your group can support his or her efforts in the legislative system.

In addition, ask who else you should be talking to. If the official supports your cause, he or she can direct you toward allies as well as legislators who could be swayed, as well as the opposition whose arguments should be analyzed for strategic purposes. Search out bipartisan supporters; Democrats and Republicans don't always fall into line on issues in the way you might expect. Having bipartisan support can help move your bill forward much more quickly.

How do you respond if your official is not enthusiastic about your cause? Start by asking about the official's concerns, and find out what information is needed to assuage those concerns. You may find that your official is absolutely not interested in supporting your work. If that's the case, make the strongest case possible for your issue, stay polite, and then wrap up the meeting.

In closing, thank the official for taking the time to meet with you and express your appreciation for the effort. If you think it would be helpful to leave behind some materials for the official's review after the meeting, come prepared with a packet of information.

STEP 4. FOLLOW UP AFTER THE MEETING.

Start by sending your official a follow-up thank-you note. If your policy maker made a promise or commitment to you, be sure to reach out again and confirm that follow-through. Likewise, if you promised to deliver more information or materials, follow through yourself. Remember, this is an initial conversation and the beginning of a relationship; just one meeting might not get you what you're looking for, so be prepared to continue the conversation.

Jessica Assaf went to the California state capitol more than four times in the process of lobbying for two pieces of legislation. This is her story.

SUCCESS STORY
THE BODY BURDEN Jessica Assaf was thirteen years old when

she read in her local newspaper that the breast cancer rates in her community had risen 60 percent in eight years. She was compelled to find the cause of the high cancer rates, so she got involved with the Marin Cancer Project. She was shocked to learn that unlike the food and drug industry, the cosmetic industry is not regulated by the Food and Drug Administration. In fact, the products individuals use on a daily basis contain toxic chemicals linked to cancer, birth defects, and infertility. In response to this problem, Jessica was one of the five founding members of Teens for Safe Cosmetics, a teen-led coalition striving to ban toxic chemicals from cosmetics and personal care products.

Over the course of four years, Teens for Safe Cosmetics hosted annual teen summits and monthly advocacy events and helped pass a proposed bill into law. Drafted by a state legislator, SB484, a bill requiring cosmetic manufacturers to disclose carcinogenic ingredients to the public, was the first piece of legislation regulating the cosmetic industry. Teens for Safe Cosmetics held press conferences and went to the state capitol four times to meet with legislators and gain support for the passage of this bill. Although the cosmetic industry spent millions of dollars in lobbying efforts to oppose the legislation, SB484 was signed into law by Governor Arnold Schwarzenegger in October of 2005.

Next, the teens returned to the state capital to lobby for the Toxic Toys Bill, to ban phthalates from children's toys and baby bottle nipples. Phthalates, which are added to plastics to make them more durable and flexible, are considered a health risk and are being phased out of products in Europe and the United States. When Jessica learned that Governor Schwarzenegger intended to veto the bill, she and her friends lobbied him directly, educating him about the health impacts. This new bill became law in October 2007. Helping pass two state laws reinforced for Jessica the idea that any individual, regardless of age or experience, can make a difference.

"Youth should know that **OFFICIALS IN CONGRESS ARE WAITING TO HEAR FROM US**. We are the 'good guys' because we are so motivated to make positive social change." **—JESSICA ASSAF**

Sometimes elected officials aren't willing to meet with you on your issue, or refuse to take action after repeated meetings. When this is the case, you can look to "bird-dogging" opportunities to embarrass them or encourage them to do the right thing in front of a wider audience.

Bird-dogging

Bird-dogging refers to attending public events where a candidate for public office or an elected representative will appear and calling on him or her to publicly address an issue, support your cause, or reconsider a stance he or she has already taken. Your bold, vocal presence at public events on the campaign trail can capture media attention and force the candidate to address your issues.

At some events the candidates will open up a "question and answer" session for the public; other times your group will have to be more forward and simply shout out your question or your message. You may not know in advance what to expect; in the beginning of the event, have one of your team members search for an event coordinator and ask whether the public will be invited to pose questions.

Prepare your team to ask focused questions about your issue that will invite a real conversation and try to get the candidate's position stated on the record in front of the media. Speaking up publicly at a rally or press conference is not for the faint of heart, so practice in advance, or give this job to the most vocal and confident members of your group. Chances are you will get only one opportunity to speak, if any, so stay on point and use your moment wisely.

To bird-dog successfully, it can be a good idea to unite your team with visuals, like posters, pins, or T-shirts. Even a small group of individuals wearing T-shirts or holding signs with a unified message and colors can help you stand out in a large crowd, particularly if the public is not given an opportunity to speak.

Creative tactics and visuals help. During the 2000 presidential campaign my friends dressed up as caped crusaders "Captain Climate" and "Boy Atmosphere," in colorful and hilarious spandex costumes, calling on Republican presidential candidate John McCain to take a stance on global warming. They captured the attention of McCain and his staff, and McCain ultimately drafted the first climate change bill brought before the Senate. Not only did the bird-dogging end up catalyzing a series of senate hearings and discussions on climate change, but also the caped crusaders were immortalized in a newspaper comic strip and multiple stories. Bird-dogging can be playful and fun while being effective!

Public Hearings

Decision-making bodies such as Congress, as well as city councils, boards of county commissioners, and planning commissions, often host opportunities to hear from constituents about particular issues. For example, a local government may hold a public hearing to gather public input on a controversial development plan. Your organizational allies should be informed about upcoming hearing dates.

State or federal legislative committees and subcommittees may solicit public testimony on a proposed piece of legislation; upcoming federal hearings are listed at www.capitolhearings.org. You will need to contact your state government offices to get details for state hearings. To find out about pending local public hearings, review your local newspaper or call your city or county government offices. These are all good opportunities to speak out in support of your issue where government officials will be present and listening.

Ask the hearing coordinators how to get on the queue to speak. Arrangements for presenting testimony vary. In some cases you may need to formally request to be added to the agenda; in others, you simply show up the day of the hearing and take a number.

Draft your speech in advance, based on the principles covered in chapter 4, Spread Your Message. Usually you will have anywhere from two to five minutes to share your views. Respect the time limit, and practice your speech to make sure it falls within the allotted time. Make your main points first, then repeat them frequently throughout your talk.

Prepare for questions. Often you won't be peppered with questions after your testimony, but you should try to predict some of the questions you could expect from the decision-making body, especially from those who oppose your perspective, and be prepared to address their concerns.

Begin by thanking the forum for the opportunity to speak. Treat your audience with respect and grace, even if you think they don't agree with you. Always share your firsthand experience. Have you been affected by pollution? Do you have asthma? Is a natural area that you used to explore as a child at risk for development? If possible, tell a personal and compelling story that connects you to the issue at hand.

You can also spark dialogue about your issue in city government forums. If your issue isn't already a hot topic, introduce a city council resolution—which will start a conversation in government bodies and, when endorsed, provide a good hook for a media announcement.

PASSING RESOLUTIONS

City council resolutions are formal expressions of support for your issue that help raise the profile of your campaign. To pass a resolution, you need to first draft one, then build support from your community, and finally get your city council members on board so they'll vote for the resolution during an upcoming meeting.

STEP 1: DRAFT YOUR RESOLUTION.

Binding resolutions affect city policies; nonbinding resolutions simply express an opinion and are easier to pass. Your campaign may be limited to asking the city to express their support for your issue; in that case, a nonbinding resolution is just fine. However, if you would like to influence city policies—for example, mandating the purchasing of green supplies or green building practices—you'll want to draft a binding resolution.

STEP 2: BUILD SUPPORT.

Using the tactics discussed in chapter 4, Spread Your Message, and chapter 8, Make Media Headlines, educate the people in your community about the benefits of a city council resolution and gather evidence of community support to present to the city council.

STEP 3: GET A CITY COUNCIL ALLY.

Research the members of your council to find out who might be willing to support or sponsor the resolution. Meet with your local city council members; start with the individuals you think will be most supportive of your work. Identify a persuasive council member to formally introduce the resolution to the council and ask him or her for strategies and ways to influence other council members who may initially be opposed to your proposal.

STEP 4: SPEAK OUT CONFIDENTLY.

At the city council meeting where the resolution will be voted on, bring lots of sympathetic community members, including individuals ready and willing to speak out on behalf of the resolution.

Although all of these tools influence elected and appointed officials, they're of little use if we don't have environmentally responsive candidates in political posts. This is particularly true when we've got legislation on the table—how do we make sure that politicians vote correctly on our issues? Well, what do our candidates care about? Votes, votes, votes! If we can prove that the youth vote helped usher them into office, we have more leverage to get them to stand strong on our issues. To do that, we've got to make sure that youth are registered to vote, getting out to the polls en masse, and voting for candidates that are interested in our issues.

GETTING OUT THE VOTE

The 2000s were a record decade for youth political participation, a reversal from the steady decline in youth voting that occurred after the Vietnam War. Young voters are no longer relegated to the margins in terms of electoral influence—and this was particularly true in the 2008 elections, in which youth exerted enormous influence over the election of Barack Obama and major shifts in Congress.

Voter outreach specialists say personal contact increases turnout among young voters by up to ten percentage points; a phone call increases turnout by up to five points, particularly when young people contact their peers! When Election Day comes around, plan to join up with your local Get Out the Vote (GOTV) effort, or launch your own, following Christina Wong's lead.

SUCCESS STORY
TAKING TO THE BATTLEGROUND Alarmed by the roll-
back of environmental protection laws, **Christina Wong** of Sacramento, California, decided to go straight to the "grassroots" of the problem in 2004. She founded a local chapter of the League of Conservation Voters (LCV) on the University of California campus at Berkeley and then expanded efforts at the University of California at Santa Cruz, the University of California at Davis, and the University of San Francisco. LCV is a nonpartisan watchdog organization that tracks elected officials' voting records on environmental issues. Christina's group led voter registration drives, coordinated

events with other student groups, and recruited students to join LCV's Environmental Victory Project.

Through her group's efforts, twenty college students volunteered to spend at least a month in battleground states registering voters and informing them about environmental issues with a goal of electing environmentally friendly candidates during the fall election. In addition to recruiting students, Christina's group took on a larger goal: to create widespread public education about the importance of presidential leadership to protect the environment. They targeted students from diverse backgrounds, not just those who had a prior interest in the environment, to become engaged in the election.

© Amanda Soosai

"IF EVERYONE HELPED OUT WITH ONE CAUSE that they believed in—the environment, health care, civil rights— THE WORLD WOULD BE IN MUCH BETTER SHAPE than it is right now." —CHRISTINA WONG

Like Christina, you can get involved in voter registration and Get Out the Vote efforts—or even start your own—at your campus or in your community. Make sure you're registered to vote first, then register your peers to vote. During election season, snag a stack of registration forms from the local post office or from the local offices of the political party you support and set up a registration station on campus or in front of your local coffee shop or youth hangouts.

Partner with other organizations, student groups, professors, and career centers to do outreach to students. Even easier, help people register online, using sites like RockTheVote.com. Set up a table (or even an ironing board) with laptops in a high-traffic area and ask folks, "Are you registered to vote?" If they're not, ask them to stop and fill out the online forms right there—it takes just a few minutes. Wherever you do outreach, make sure you have handouts with additional ways to get involved.

On Election Day, show up at your peers' doors or give them a call, reminding them of their polling place. And get ready to celebrate your GOTV victories as election night ends!

If getting other people elected isn't your cup of tea, how about running for office yourself? More than half of all members of Congress, governors, and U.S. presidents were elected to office for the first time before they were thirty-six years of age. Elected officials under thirty-six represent nearly 5 percent of all congressional, gubernatorial, legislative, and city and county commission seats in the United States. These folks help set policy, direct billions of dollars of public monies, and set the direction of our nation's progress for years to come.

STEPPING INTO OFFICE

Formal bodies may be open to youth representation, including the local parks and recreation board, the planning commission, the environmental commission, the energy commission, the board of education or school board, and the city council.

Some of these are appointed positions; contact your city or county government offices to find out when and how to apply. Other positions are elected; you will need to run a compelling campaign to be elected to office. Running a winning campaign can be a challenge, so it's a good idea to seek out successful youth officials as mentors, as well as organizations that train and support young candidates (listed at the end of this chapter) to support your efforts.

If your local government lacks a council, commission, or taskforce for the environment, encourage them to set one up. Many cities and counties are creating new bodies to deal with various environmental issues—for example, creating an energy and environment commission, a local foods commission, or a climate action council. These can be vitally important venues to steer your local institutions, neighborhoods, cities, and counties on the path toward sustainability.

When Ariana Katovich was in college at U.C. Santa Barbara, she was running a student environmental organization, working part-time, and attending school full-time when she decided to run for office. She was elected to her local park and recreation district, through sheer energy and determination. Here she shares her winning strategy for getting elected to office, and some tips for a GOTV effort.

SUCCESS STORY
ARIANA KATOVICH'S GUIDE TO TURNING OUT VOTERS AND GETTING ELECTED

Know the issues! I talked to people on "my" side and the "other" side, read the board minutes of the Park and Recreation District, attended board meetings, went on site visits, and started taking notes on improvements I could make to our current system.

Build coalitions. I built coalitions with the larger campaigns at that time, including campaigns for county supervisor, assembly members, and Congress, and walked door-to-door with them. We had a combined ticket, which helped increase my exposure. My volunteers walked for them and their volunteers walked for me. The larger campaigns have more resources, but local campaigns have a lot of grassroots energy. The large and local can work wonders together!

Seek endorsements. I had local celebrities, newspapers, campus groups, and organizations endorse my candidacy.

Fundraise. I wrote letters to my family, friends, and organizations. Make sure you have enough money to host events, print your flyers, and buy your volunteers pizza. Lots of people also have talents they can share for free or at a very low cost if they believe in your work. Network and be open to using people's pro bono services!

Make awesome signs. My voting demographic was college students and Democratic voters. I had my signs silkscreened by a great artist; people loved them and put them up in their windows, on their refrigerators, and on their walls. In addition, students love "guerilla marketing"—marketing based on creativity and energy, rather than the big bucks. People just don't trust the slick glossy yard signs. My volunteers hand-painted signs and put them up everywhere. I also painted big wooden sandwich board–style signs and chained them wherever it was allowed.

Debate on the issues. Prepare yourself for debate, and practice your talking points out loud, over and over again. Ask friends to quiz you. My strategy was to be better educated on the issues than my opponents. Any time you attend public events, dress nicely.

Treat your volunteers like gold. I called potential volunteers myself, asking them to volunteer and thanking them for their help. Aside from saying "thanks" (a lot), make sure they have food, drink, and music while they work. Your volunteers should be clear on who you are and what you stand for, so if they represent you, they know what to say and have an understanding of your good intentions. Then set up lot of phone banks in advance of Election Day and call every potential voter to remind them to get out to the polls. If your state relies heavily on voting by mail, make sure you are reaching out to potential voters far in advance of Election Day.

Register those voters while you can! We blasted music, set up tables all over campus, and even worked with the residence halls to do a nonpartisan GOTV drive. When the freshmen moved into the dorms, we worked with each residence hall to send volunteers to the orientation meeting each floor had with their residence assistant and passed out GOTV forms.

Class talks. Although you can't go into each class and say "vote for me," with the blessings of the professors you can pass out voter registration cards. We made transparencies of a correctly filled-out form, passed out the forms to the big lecture halls, and walked people through the registration process.

Throw a concert. How do you get your voters together? Show them a good time! I used my campaign funds to hire local bands and rent the amphitheater, and three thousand people attended. It was fun and great publicity for my campaign.

Letters to the editor. Some say the letters to the editor section is one of the most-read sections of the paper. Aside from getting the papers to endorse you, ask your volunteers and supporters to write a short letter about why they are voting for you. We also had people submit cartoons to keep the message fresh, new, and interesting!

On Election Day, be prepared to not sleep. Gather your volunteers early. Show them the battle plan, give them a huge breakfast, and send them to walk (and rewalk) their section of the neighborhood, getting people out to vote. We had a "Go Vote" parade, drove around with megaphones in cars and on bikes, had a rally on campus, and even had our dogs wear our campaign T-shirts!

Give away prizes for voting. We partnered with the local burrito shop to give a free burrito to anyone with a voting stub, regardless of political affiliation.

Election party. Get ready to celebrate your hard work (and, you hope, victory) and make sure every volunteer who has ever worked on your campaign knows where it is happening!

"Build coalitions. Larger campaigns have more resources, but **LOCAL CAMPAIGNS** have a lot of **GRASSROOTS ENERGY!**" —ARIANA KATOVICH

Operating through political channels isn't a panacea for solving all of our environmental challenges, but it's certainly a critical part of the package. If you are frustrated with how your political system has failed to address the needs of the general public, you're not alone. Many youth are tired of a system polluted by dirty money, election fraud, and corporate lobbyists. But keep your chin up! According to Rock the Vote, there are forty-four million potential young voters (ages eighteen to twenty-nine) in the United States—making up more than one-fifth of the electorate. Youth have enormous collective power to elect officials that represent our positions—and to hold officials accountable to advancing an environmental agenda that resonates with our demographic. Together we can become a dominant political force to reshape American politics and advance a strong environmental agenda.

NEXT STOP: CORPORATE CAMPAIGNS

If we wait for our government to regulate corporate behavior, we can end up waiting a long time. Even when regulations are on the books, sometimes companies break rules because it's easier (and cheaper) to pay the fines than to engage in environmentally friendlier practices. Thankfully, there's another alternative to letting our governments change companies: we create the public pressure and incentive for corporations to change. The next chapter will show you how to run a corporate campaign, shining the spotlight directly on these companies so they aren't let off the hook.

RESOURCES

Apathy Is Boring, www.apathyisboring.com Apathy Is Boring is a Canadian nonpartisan project that uses art and technology to educate youth about democracy.

Democracy for America Campaign Academy, www.dfalink.com Consultants with decades of experience give youth the skills to run a winning campaign. Topics include field planning, voter contact, fundraising, communications, volunteer recruitment, and more.

Front Line Leaders Academy, www.youngpeoplefor.org The Front Line Leaders Academy, hosted by Young People For, gives young prospective candidates and campaign leaders the ability to learn from successful political campaign professionals.

League of Young Voters, www.theleague.com The League of Young Voters empowers young people nationwide to participate in the democratic process and create progressive political change at the local, state, and national level—with a focus on noncollege youth and youth from low-income communities and communities of color.

PolitiCorps Fellows, www.politicorps.org PolitiCorps is a political boot camp consisting of hands-on skills training, public policy intensives, and real-world applications of leadership skills and campaign savvy.

Project Vote Smart, www.votesmart.org Project Vote Smart is a nonpartisan organization that collects and disseminates information to the general public on the issue positions and legislative votes of all elected officials and candidates for office.

Rock the Vote, www.rockthevote.com Rock the Vote uses music, popular culture, and new technologies to engage and incite young people to register and vote in every election, as well as tools to leverage their power in the political process.

Wellstone Action, www.wellstone.org Wellstone Action is a national training center for people interested in progressive change. They help activists win on issues and elect progressive candidates by training them in the nuts and bolts of grassroots organizing, voter engagement, political advocacy, and leadership development.

06
CORPORATE CAMPAIGNS

USE YOUR CONSUMER POWER TO GREEN BUSINESSES

I mmediately after graduating from college, I worked on the Heritage Forests Campaign, an alliance of organizations and individuals committed to permanently protecting nearly sixty million acres of the last wild forests within the U.S. Forest System. Our alliance gathered more than 1.5 million public comments in support of protecting these forests, and ultimately persuaded President Bill Clinton to issue an executive order, popularly called the "Roadless Rule," to protect these areas. Days after the Roadless Rule was signed into law, Boise Cascade, one of the nation's largest loggers in old-growth forests, filed a legal challenge to overturn the rule.

I began to see clearly then how corporations can undermine American democracy. More than 95 percent of the public comments generated during the Heritage Forests Campaign—at that time the largest public comment response seen on any issue in American history—were in support of protecting the forests. These forests belonged to the public, as part of the U.S. Forest System, and the public wanted to see them off-limits to logging.

Yet a corporation was able to play a critical role in overturning the rule. Boise Cascade's actions weren't an anomaly. Natural resources that serve as the foundation of our survival as a human species—like clean air, clean water, and arable land—are increasingly at risk from corporate abuse.

A number of companies, accountable only to shareholders, pay scant attention to environmental concerns—or even actively work against environmental protections. Corporations often use their political influence in the form of trade associations, lobbyists, and political donations to overturn laws that protect natural resources while promoting and supporting unsustainable environmental policies that allow them to make huge profits.

After my time with the Heritage Forests Campaign, I became interested in new strategies to protect forests. I went on to work for three years with Rainforest Action Network, an organization that uses corporate or "markets" campaigns to pressure companies to act in the public interest. Corporate campaigns put pressure on a particular company to change its practices. Often a win from one of the biggest and most influential companies in an industry can create a domino effect, with the other companies in the industry following suit.

In addition to campaigning against destructive corporate practices, we need to support companies with good environmental practices. We all need food and various products and services to carry out our lives. Most of our consumer needs are supplied by companies. We can vote with our dollars when we purchase local, organic food and recycled products. Just as important, we need a new generation of business leaders to find more ways to generate clean energy, produce green products, and grow and distribute sustainable food. If today's corporate leaders won't listen, then it's time to replace them. We can use our creativity and innovation to solve major challenges and create a new, green economy.

GO AFTER THE BIG BRANDS

Ready to make change in the corporate sector? Maybe you think the U.S. automotive industry needs an overhaul, to start turning out greener, more fuel-efficient vehicles. Or you can't stand that the bottled water industry produces up to 1.5 million tons of plastic waste per year. (Plus, the industry requires up to forty-seven million gallons of oil per year to produce the bottles, not to mention the fuel to ship the bottles around the world!) What can you do to help transform an entire industry of global players?

Well, quite a lot, actually. Some big wins have occurred because of corporate campaigns, often student and youth-driven. Here are some examples:

➤ Food and Water Watch mobilized activists to make thousands of emails and phone calls and host rallies pressuring Starbucks to serve only 100-percent hormone-free milk in all of its U.S. stores. In 2007, Food and Water Watch won, and the CEO of Starbucks cited citizen activism as the primary impetus for the company's commitment.

➤ Rainforest Action Network realized that many environmentally destructive projects could be stopped if they could cut off the funding pipeline directly from the big banks. Citigroup, the number one lender to the coal industry and fossil-fuel pipelines worldwide, was their first target. Students held protests at bank branches and encouraged clients to cut up their credit cards. Thanks to their efforts, in 2004 Citigroup became the first bank to adopt a comprehensive environmental policy to guide its lending practices.

➤ Victoria's Secret had a "dirty little secret" of printing catalogues on paper that was originally from forests in endangered caribou habitat, according to ForestEthics. In 2006, after years of flamboyant protests where youth dressed up in lingerie and poked fun at the company, Limited Brands (the parent company of Victoria's Secret) announced they would no longer get their paper from pulp sourced from caribou habitat.

Each of these big companies—Starbucks, Citigroup, Victoria's Secret—needs to attract youth customers, particularly college students, to their products and services. Young people are a prime marketing demographic for many big brands, particularly those selling soft drinks, packaged foods, credit cards and student loans, clothing, music, cell phones, and handheld electronics. When a company wins your loyalty before its competitors do, you're likely to become a customer for life. For this reason, when you organize with your peers, you have enormous power to influence corporate practices. The last thing a company that markets to youth wants is a tarnished reputation with that very demographic.

So what do you do with this power? You might decide you're not going to buy their products, but a personal boycott is unlikely to make a huge dent in their quarterly sales. You can spread the word, producing consumer guides. Customers won't know what companies are up to unless you educate them. Pamphlets, guides, and "report cards" that give grades based on environmental and social criteria all can help your community members know more about "voting" with their dollars. But organizing a campaign targeting the company is your best chance for lasting impact. Although you may think your local group is too small to have any impact on a big company, May Boeve's story demonstrates otherwise.

SUCCESS STORY
THE ROAD TO DETROIT May Boeve, twenty-one, and friends led Middlebury College's action-oriented environmental and social justice group, the Sunday Night Group. After May attended a conference on building the grassroots climate change movement, she put the conference's message into action.

In the summer of 2005, May and seven other students embarked on The Road to Detroit, a fifteen-thousand-mile road trip around the country in a vegetable-oil-and-biodiesel-fueled bus. May and company toured concerts, festivals, and community events to spread the word that cleaner air and a stable climate are possible.

More than eleven thousand people supported their Clean Car Pledge, promising to buy a U.S. union-made, fuel-efficient vehicle as soon as it became available. The tour culminated in Detroit, where May and the crew delivered these signatures to a representative of the United Auto Workers. Two months later, Ford announced it would increase the production of hybrid vehicles tenfold each year until 2012.

© Drew Altizer

"Many corporations appeal to the youth market—and **THIS IS A SOURCE OF POWER FOR YOUNG PEOPLE.** We can use our consumer power to force changes in destructive company policies." **—MAY BOEVE**

Ford did not make the announcement solely because of the work of May and her peers; national groups were running a "Jumpstart Ford" campaign, using media pressure, nonviolent direct action, and public outreach to change Ford's practices. But the work of small, regionally based groups (like May's) was a crucial part of building public pressure across the nation, particularly in Ford's hometown. Like May, to be successful at targeting industry giants, you'll want to join forces with an existing national boycott or campaign (or launch a new effort with a wide network of student groups across the nation). In the Resources section at the close of this chapter, you can find some of the organizations that run nationwide corporate campaigns—start by checking out their efforts. In addition, many of the student and youth networks detailed in chapter 11, Change the World, also run corporate campaigns.

The rest of this chapter will teach you how to launch your own corporate campaign for locally based or small businesses.

THINK GLOBAL, ACT LOCAL

Although the efforts of a few dozen or a few hundred individuals in your city may be unlikely to influence a multimillion- or multibillion-dollar company headquartered far away, those same individuals can make a big impact on locally based companies and small businesses.

What can you do if you discover that a local power plant is contributing to higher rates of asthma in your town? Or your favorite local restaurant fails to recycle, even though there's a recycling plant in town? What if the neighborhood supermarket is selling Chilean sea bass, an endangered species, when more sustainable alternatives are available? Here's a step-by-step guide to launching a corporate campaign.

STEP 1: CHOOSE YOUR COMPANY.

There are a number of companies you could choose, but you have limited time and resources. You should pick just one company at a time, even if a number are involved in poor environmental practices. It's a good idea to start with a local company or store. Examine these questions as you're choosing which company to influence:

Which business is doing the most harm? Media coverage and public sympathy are earned most easily when you're going after the biggest and most harmful business.

Who's a leader? You might look for a leader in the industry (the first grocery store to introduce organic food in your town) or a community-oriented business (a hardware store that is consistently in the news for local giving and involvement). Leaders are typically concerned about their image and are often innovators in the business community. If they are already innovators (even on issues unrelated to the environment), they may be more open to adopting green business practices as well.

Who's concerned with their public image? Some companies don't care much about how they're perceived by the public. This is particularly true for companies that don't rely on a walk-in or word-of-mouth customer base. You want to find a company that seems responsive to consumer pressure. Companies that invest in advertising are more likely to be responsive to corporate campaigns, whether we're talking about a local business taking out ads in the local daily paper or a national apparel company featured in glossy magazines.

Is any of their staff or management concerned about environmental issues? Does the company project an eco-friendly image (even if their operations aren't up to par)?

STEP 2: SET YOUR DEMANDS.

Remember the SMART goals you set while drafting your plan in chapter 2, Create an Action Plan? You want to model your demands in the same way. Asking a business to be "environmentally sound" is awfully vague. Asking a business, instead, to "stop purchasing old-growth wood products and remove all existing old-growth wood products from store shelves within twelve months" is specific, measurable, and timely (only the company can determine whether it's achievable and realistic). Look at their competitors' environmental practices—asking them to meet or beat the best practices in their industry is often a good start.

STEP 3: WHO'S YOUR TARGET?

Within the company, who has the power to make the change: the business owner, a purchasing director, or a manager? Are there any sympathetic individuals in the company? Do they have a community relations department or an environmental department? For smaller companies and local businesses, the founder, owner, or managing director will likely be the decision maker.

What if you want to convince a company to invest in setting up a "sustainability" department? You might choose to target the human resources team members, responsible for employment and recruiting, along with the head of the company. If you want a company to stop buying certain products that are produced in an unsustainable manner, you may choose to target the purchasing team members, who are responsible for sourcing products and supplies for the company.

As you are selecting your targets, look at what access you have to reach and influence those individuals. What place of worship do they frequent, where do they live, where do they recreate, who do they donate money to, what college did they graduate from, and where do they speak publicly? When organizers at Rainforest Action Network were targeting Citi's destructive banking investments, they discovered that the CEO was about to speak at his alma mater. They worked with dozens of students to prepare tough questions about Citi's environmental record for the question-and-answer portion of his talk. Rather than receiving a warm welcome on campus, the CEO was put on the spot to defend his company's actions. Search for these types of opportunities to influence the decision makers.

STEP 4: MAKE CONTACT.

Make first contact with a formal letter to your target, laying out your concerns and your demands and asking for a meeting. If your target won't meet with you directly, try to meet with someone next in line in decision-making power on your issue. Prepare for the meeting in much the same way that you prepare for a lobby meeting (see page 80). You'll want to address your concerns about the company's practices and present your demand set. Make a strong argument for why the company should adopt these practices: why and how are their customers concerned about the environment, and how will adopting green practices help the company in the marketplace? Companies rarely do something because it's the "right thing to do"; rather, they respond to their customers' concerns. You have to do some basic research to figure out who their customers are and how to demonstrate that their customers would like to see these changes.

This meeting is also an opportunity for you to gather information about the company: ask them to tell you about their company's environmental policies, how they have been addressing the issue, and whether it's possible for them to meet your demands. If the answer is no, ask whether there are any particular obstacles standing in the way of the company's improving their environmental operations and meeting your demands. Ideally, leave the meeting with a timeline for action and next steps.

Remember: your target is not your enemy! Start off trying to look for shared values and beliefs and leave your accusations at home. You may not want to use the term "demands," for example, during your first meetings. Instead, you can position your demands as a set of suggested improvements for the company. This first meeting is your opportunity to learn about the company and its employees and figure out how to best work with them— or if need be, pressure them from the outside—to make the changes our planet needs. Even if a company doesn't make a promise to move toward sustainability in the first meeting, it may be unwise to launch a campaign the very next week.

You'll always have the opportunity to escalate tactics later, but in the beginning, look for positive incentives for the company to make changes and ways you can help them do so. You'll be much more successful if you are able to find at least one ally within the company to champion your cause, and you are obviously far more likely to find an internal champion when you approach a company from the framework of being a partner in their journey toward sustainability, rather than a thorn in their side. Plus, you will look unreasonable if you attack a company publicly without giving them some time to respond to your concerns.

MOSQUITO IN THE TENT

What do you do if a company refuses to meet with you or absolutely refuses to change their operations? Well, then it's time to be the mosquito in the tent: the small but constant and persistent pest that keeps pressuring them to make changes. You can employ a range of tactics to pressure companies big and small to change their practices, including letter-writing or sign-on letters, guerilla advertising, product boycotts, media attention, street theater outside their doors, protests, and meetings with the decision makers, to name a few.

Before you select your tactics, determine which elements of their business model you can influence. Can you affect their customers, their potential employees, their advertising and brand image, or some other crucial element of the business? Each of these may require different tactics. Influencing customers is often most easily done at storefront locations by distributing flyers or hosting protests. If they are a huge employer in the area, you may choose tactics to tarnish the company's reputation at local job fairs or on-campus recruiting events: this may deter recent graduates from taking a position with the company. If your aim is to tarnish their brand reputation, you may use media outreach and guerilla advertising, instead. You have many options, but be strategic in choosing the tactic that will actually get to the company's Achilles' heel—what do you think you can influence, and what will persuade the company to make change?

Before going public with your first tactic, inform the decision maker that you are preparing to launch a campaign targeting their company. Sometimes the threat of a public campaign is enough to get them to take action.

Sign-on Letters

Launching a sign-on letter from community members shows the company that it's not just a handful of isolated activists who are concerned. You can also do an institutional sign-on letter, asking the heads of schools, environmental organizations, businesses, and churches to sign on in support. Each one of these individuals, when signing on for his or her group, is speaking for dozens or hundreds of other individuals, too! This is a great tool to educate and build alliances with new groups—you may well need their support as you continue the campaign.

Sever Business Ties

So an unsavory business is operating where you go to school? Organize a campaign to kick them off campus. If there are environmentally negligent companies with operations, stores, or products on your campus, research what contracts or formal arrangements your school has made with the company. What are the provisions and length of the contract, and who at your campus makes final decisions about extending the contract? Begin to research the company's competitors who have better environmental records, to see whether they can match or better the existing contractual terms. If you can match or approach the contractual terms, meet with the campus administration and make a case for shifting providers. Just make sure the new company has better environmental operations than the present company!

Of course, while you're doing this behind-the-scenes research, you need to be concurrently building campus support for a shift in vendors. If you are not able to point to strong student support for your work, it will likely be challenging to convince the administration to invest in the effort (and potential cost) of setting up new contracts with other companies. Administrators often use excuses like "the contract binds us to work with this company for so-and-so many years" or "it's too expensive to change" to wiggle out of taking responsibility. What if that's true? Truth is, part of your role at the campus is to make it sustainable, and if the administration lacks a process to evaluate sustainability before signing a contract with a company, your efforts will help them develop a process for doing so.

Shareholder Activism

Your campus is investing funds in the company? Get your campus to shift funds elsewhere, or engage in *shareholder activism*: using the power of stock ownership to promote environmental and social change. It's a relatively new strategy, first gaining international attention in the 1980s when investors were pressured to drop stocks of companies operating in South Africa during the racial segregation and discrimination of apartheid. As more and more companies left South Africa, eventually the economic pressure was one of the forces that helped end apartheid.

So just what is shareholder activism? It can take many forms. Shareholder resolutions are nonbinding proposals—suggestions for a change in operations—submitted by shareholders addressing the company's operations. Even though the proposal is nonbinding, which means the company isn't required to act on the proposal, the media attention and public scrutiny generated during the act of promoting the resolution (and voting) can be very beneficial for your cause.

Shareholder meetings are another great opportunity to take your issue public—these meetings are annual events where the company allows shareholders to pose questions and vote on select company operations. Even if you don't own stock yourself, you can find a shareholder who will give you their space as a "proxy" representative. These events are ripe opportunities to pose difficult questions inside the meeting, vote on shareholder resolutions introduced by your activist group, and supplement any activism outside the meeting, such as a protest, with an inside strategy.

Protest Their Recruiters

If the company comes to your campus to recruit for jobs or summer internships, you can counter-protest, hand out your protest information, or put the recruiter on the spot by asking tough questions publicly about the company's environmental record. Consider using one of the ideas detailed in chapter 7, Protest with Power.

Culture Jamming and Subvertising

Companies spend lots of money to develop and spread a particular brand image. You can rebrand a company by recrafting their logos and product images with a slight twist, or launching a website with a similar web address that informs the public of the company's environmental and social misdoings. Check out AdBusters (www.adbusters.org) or the Yes Men (www.theyesmen.org) for great examples of culture jamming.

Adopt a Store

If the company you are targeting has retail operations locally, adopt a store—commit to being a constant presence until the company improves their green practices. You can hold protests outside of the store, write letters to the local newspaper, take over the store in a short march, or hand out educational materials in front of the store to their customers, until you're asked to leave by management. If the store offers credit cards, get consumers to cut up their cards and return them to the company with a note of concern about the company's environmental practices. The possibilities are limitless!

Not in Our Backyard

Your campaign doesn't always have to shift a company's existing practices—you can use corporate campaigns to stop a company from launching a new, unwanted operation or location in your community. Public education, media activism, and public protests can all be used to halt the project, as Erica Fernandez demonstrated in California.

SUCCESS STORY
NOT IN OUR NEIGHBORHOOD Erica Fernandez moved to

the California coast from Mexico when she was just ten years old. A few years later, she found out that a liquefied natural gas (LNG) facility was proposed for the coast of Oxnard and Malibu, with a thirty-six-inch pipeline routed through low-income neighborhoods. Natural gas is considered a cleaner form of fossil fuel than coal, but it has its own dangers: the pollution of water during drilling, the possibility of leaks during transport, and air pollution at the power plants. Erica worked in concert with the Sierra Club and Latino No on LNG group to mobilize the youth and Latino voice in protests and public meetings. She organized weekly protests at the BHP Billiton offices in Oxnard, met regularly with community members, marched through neighborhoods that would be most affected, reached out to the media, and brought more than 250 high school students to a critical rally.

When the California State Lands Commission met to vote on the project, her passionate testimony helped convince the commission to deny the project. Next, she spoke to convince the California Coastal Commission to vote 12-0 against the project, and she worked on a letter-writing and phone call campaign to the governor asking him to veto the project, just as the commissioners did. Erica's community organizing and dogged determination played a crucial role in helping her community resist a multinational billion-dollar corporation.

"This project could be a model because **WE BROUGHT TOGETHER DIFFERENT COMMUNITIES** to fight together against a very dangerous project. This is what made us so successful." **—ERICA FERNANDEZ**

Erica's campaign was long and grueling. Although it lasted for four years, people didn't give up hope, and Erica and friends were a constant presence at the BHP Billiton offices. In addition, although it started with a small number of individuals, ultimately thousands of individuals attended key public protests. As you can see, campaigns targeting multinational, multimillion-dollar (or multibillion-dollar!) companies can be lengthy and demanding affairs, but it's not impossible for a small group of persistent individuals to go up against big companies. In this case, Erica couldn't appeal to the company itself to change its practices—she had to target other decision makers that could halt or change the company's practices, like the State Lands and Coastal Commissions.

CREATE A GREEN ECONOMY

Still not satisfied with corporate America? Then maybe it's time to create something better. Many companies are working to create a green and fair economy. Some companies are creating innovative clean technology to solve issues in energy, water, and waste; others are installing clean energy technologies and retrofitting buildings to be more efficient. We need new leaders to drive the transition to a green economy. One place to start is getting a green education. Some schools, like the Bainbridge Graduate Institute (www.bgi.edu), now offer advanced degrees in sustainable business.

By engaging in corporate campaigns, you can not only help improve one company's practices but also help elevate the entire industry standard. Again, once you bring about changes in one big company, other companies in the industry could follow suit. As a result of Rainforest Action Network's campaign against Citigroup, for example, the company set new industry standards guiding its lending practices, a step many other banks have since taken.

Corporate campaigns can also serve as amazing educational tools. Most companies just love to advertise their green tendencies; if a company makes an environmental commitment, they're likely to share the news. That's free environmental education to all of their customers. Cool, huh? Stores in your town see thousands of shoppers annually; larger companies might educate millions. Let's say your local store, as a result of your campaign, performs an energy audit and replaces all of its lighting with energy-efficient bulbs. Then the store advertises both the cost savings and the green philosophy behind the retrofit. Shoppers who have never thought about an energy audit are now learning how a company saved money—some shoppers will take this knowledge back into their own homes and businesses and do the same.

You never know what impact your campaign will have, but chances are good that you'll influence more than just the company itself. By getting involved in corporate campaigning, you can help make structural changes to a system that's much larger than the individual—and go beyond voting with your dollars.

NEXT STOP: PROTEST WITH POWER

When decision makers won't respond to our efforts to demonstrate widespread support for the adoption of new business practices, laws, and greening projects, we have the choice to turn up the heat with protests. Communities that are shut out of positions of power or lack direct access to decision makers—the poor and working class, indigenous and native nations, immigrants, people of color, and youth, for example—often use public protests to advance their environmental concerns, particularly when earlier tactics such as letter-writing, petitions, and meetings fail to bring about campaign demands. The next chapter dives into how to use peaceful protests to advance environmental change.

RESOURCES

Corporate Accountability International, www.stopcorporateabuse .org Corporate Accountability International has been waging winning campaigns to challenge corporate abuse for more than thirty years, targeting industries like big tobacco, fast food, and bottled water.

Forest Ethics, www.forestethics.org Forest Ethics runs hard-hitting and highly effective campaigns that leverage public dialogue and pressure to combat forest destruction and climate change.

Green America, www.greenamericatoday.org Green America works to empower individuals to make purchasing and investing choices that promote social justice and environmental sustainability while demanding an end to corporate irresponsibility through collective economic action.

Green For All, www.greenforall.org Green For All is a national organization working to build an inclusive green economy strong enough to lift people out of poverty.

Organic Consumers Association (OCA), www.organicconsumers.org The OCA deals with crucial issues of food safety, industrial agriculture, genetic engineering, children's health, corporate accountability, fair trade, environmental sustainability, and other key topics, from the perspective of organic and socially responsible consumers.

People for the Ethical Treatment of Animals (PETA), www.peta.org PETA is the largest animal rights organization in the world. The group focuses on the four areas in which the largest numbers of animals suffer the most intensely for the longest periods of time: on factory farms, in laboratories, in the clothing trade, and in the entertainment industry.

Rainforest Action Network, www.ran.org Rainforest Action Network campaigns for the forests, their inhabitants, and the natural systems that sustain life by transforming the global marketplace through education, grassroots organizing, and nonviolent direct action.

Responsible Endowments Coalition, www.endowmentethics.org The Responsible Endowments Coalition works to promote responsible investment at colleges and universities in the United States.

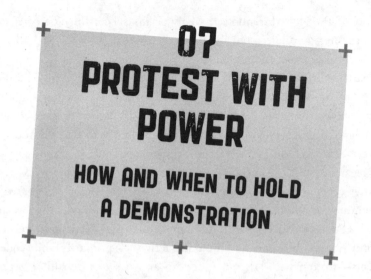

07
PROTEST WITH POWER

HOW AND WHEN TO HOLD A DEMONSTRATION

I n the past century, youth protests have been behind some of the biggest environmental, human rights, and social justice victories worldwide. Don't believe me? Here's an amazing story of youth creating monumental societal changes using peaceful protests.

Leading up to the 1960s, African-Americans were not allowed to share taxis or public transportation with whites, enter buildings through the same entrances, eat at the same restaurants, or use the same water fountains. They were often not allowed into public libraries, zoos, or parks. Youth protesters consistently and bravely put pressure on the federal government to end segregation and establish voting rights for African-Americans.

In 1960, four African-American students from a North Carolina college sat down at a segregated lunch counter in a Woolworth's in Greensboro and were refused service. The next day, the students brought twenty-seven additional protesters to join them. Each day, new students from two colleges and a high school joined, until their numbers swelled to three hundred peaceful protesters. The Greensboro sit-ins inspired a number of other sit-ins across the nation, making media headlines and winning the verbal support of President Eisenhower. Many sit-ins successfully desegregated lunch counters and later contributed to the desegregation of art galleries, beaches, parks, pools, and more.

Youth continued organizing in the Freedom Rides in 1961, in which young African-Americans and older white allies traveled together on public buses from Washington, D.C., to Jackson, Mississippi, to challenge segregation laws. Though twenty-seven Freedom Riders were arrested and sentenced to sixty days on a prison farm, ultimately buses and train stations were desegregated.

After years of growing citizen outrage, the Civil Rights Act passed in the summer of 1964, outlawing racial segregation and extending voting rights to African-Americans. At the same time, the Mississippi Freedom Summer project rallied nearly a thousand activists—primarily white college students—to join with African-American activists to teach in "Freedom Schools" and register southern voters. When these volunteers saw firsthand the challenges African-Americans faced in registering to vote or actually voting (such as bogus literacy tests), they put pressure on the government to eradicate these barriers, leading to the Voting Rights Act of 1965.

So what is a story from the civil rights movement in the 1960s doing in a book about environmental change in the new millennium? It's heartening proof of the fact that youth have a tremendous amount of power to influence any issue when they band together and demand change. The role of youth is often overshadowed by the stories of the adults in these movements: we've all heard of Rosa Parks and Martin Luther King Jr., right? But have you heard of David Leinhail Richmond or Joseph Alfred McNeil, two of the original students from the Greensboro sit-in? Without the help of the twenty-five-and-under set, the civil rights movement wouldn't have advanced as powerfully or quickly as it did.

That's the case for the environmental movement today; youth are driving major environmental victories by engaging in peaceful protests. Take Alberta Nells, for starters.

SUCCESS STORY

SAVE THE PEAKS

Alberta Nells, a sixteen-year-old from the Navajo Nation, lived near the San Francisco Peaks, an area held sacred by more than thirteen Native American Nations. A local ski resort, Arizona Snowbowl, operated on the San Francisco Peaks and requested an expansion of the resort, involving the removal of seventy-four acres of trees and use of treated sewage water to create artificial snow. When the U.S. Forest Service approved the company's plans, Alberta knew she had to step forward to stop the desecration of this sacred site. She helped launched a youth group called Youth of the Peaks to work with a related group, Save the Peaks. Youth of the Peaks started small, with just five people meeting in a local coffee shop. It steadily grew over time to include supporters from both Native American and non-Native American communities throughout the country.

Alberta and her friends organized demonstrations and marches at the foot of the resort to educate tourists about the issues surrounding the resort expansion. Each event that Youth of the Peaks hosted drew more and more supporters; Alberta and her friends used song and prayer during the protests to voice their concerns for the site and to maintain their cultural traditions. One march brought out three hundred community supporters. Eventually, the 9th Circuit Court ruled in favor of Save the Peaks, rejecting the expansion plans. Without the power of the youth voices, Save the Peaks might not have been able to generate enough public support to stop the expansion. The company continued to fight, appealing the court decision, but Alberta's team also continued to oppose the proposal.

"You **CANNOT BE AFRAID TO LET YOUR VOICE BE HEARD.** They say that the youth are the leaders of tomorrow. So we show them that we are not alone. We have our brothers and sisters with us." **—ALBERTA NELLS**

© Drew Altizer

Why did Alberta decide to use protests as a part of her campaign? As I mentioned in the previous chapter, communities shut out of decision-making processes often turn to protests when earlier calls for change fall upon deaf ears. Even if you don't call the shots from a formal decision-making position, you are not powerless. You have an enormous ability to influence those individuals in positions of power, and sometimes using confrontation is the most likely way to win a campaign.

Martin Luther King Jr. said in his book *Why We Can't Wait*, "Direct action is not a substitute for work in the courts and halls of government. Bringing about passage of a new and broad law in Congress or pleading cases in the courts of the land does not eliminate the necessity for bringing about the mass dramatization of injustice in front of city hall. Indeed, direct action and legal action complement each other; when skillfully employed, each becomes more effective." Alberta found that she could educate the public and recruit new supporters at the same time she captured the attention of her target through protests and the resulting media attention. While they fought in the courtroom, they built public pressure outside the courthouse walls. That said, protests are most effective as part of an escalation of tactics: turning up the heat over time on a target.

WHEN TO PROTEST

Confrontational tactics are not the best way to launch a campaign. Protests require a lot of time and energy to be successful, as well as an established base of supporters. Why shouldn't you jump right in with a protest to kick off your campaign? Consider this example: your mayor is considering paving over a local park to expand city parking. If your first step is inviting the media to cover a protest in front of your mayor's office, you're already shutting down a lot of opportunities for dialogue. City officials may tell the media that you failed to use official channels for feedback, and then the media may pose some difficult questions about why you chose to use a protest instead of meeting with the city staff. And if you fail to educate the public about the cons of the project, they may not understand why you are protesting.

Let's consider a different situation: you launch your campaign by doing public education, hosting public forums, and gathering petition signatures from peers and park neighbors. Ultimately, if you escalate your campaign and plan a protest, you can make a good case that you first tried other alternatives. You can tell the media and the public, "We wish we didn't have to do this, but our mayor has resisted all of our earlier attempts at dialogue.

She turned down our requests for a meeting, failed to respond to a petition signed by more than five hundred community members, and refused to speak at our community parks' forum. If the mayor won't join us for a conversation about this important issue, we'll bring our community's requests straight to her door." By demonstrating a good-faith effort to first reach your target using less confrontational tactics, you can win public and media support. As activists building movements for victory, we need all the public and media support we can garner!

Many youth-led environmental campaigns have been won using a combination of tactics like letter-writing campaigns, phone-in days, media outreach, and teach-ins (see chapter 4, Spread Your Message; chapter 5, Politics; and chapter 8, Make Media Headlines). When those tactics fail to win your demands, then it may be time to plan a protest.

If you're considering protest tactics, think carefully about the pros and cons of a protest at this point in your campaign. Does this protest align with your action plan strategy, and is it likely to influence the decision maker in your favor? Will you win more support from the public, or are you likely to alienate the very people you need on your side? Are there any risks of arrest, or expulsion or suspension from school? If so, are you prepared to deal with the repercussions, and are those risks worth it? Is your entire group comfortable with the level of risk involved with the protest? If your group can answer important questions like these and is convinced that a protest is a strategic choice at this stage in the campaign, go for it!

HOW TO PROTEST

When it's the right time to turn up the heat, the following are tried-and-true protest tactics that youth have used to demonstrate their power and win campaigns. This chapter shares when to use each tactic, how to plan them, and success stories from youth campaigns.

Demonstrations

Demonstrations (*demos* for short) are often held outside the doors of your target—in front of your campus administration's office, for example, or in front of the regional Environmental Protection Agency office. If you are working on a place-based campaign, like protecting a beach from offshore oil drilling, you can host the demo on-site.

To pick the location for your demonstration, revisit the ultimate goal of your action plan and your decision maker. Whose vote, decision, or action are you trying to influence? There's no single "correct" choice; in fact, you may find yourself with many potential targets. Let's look at an example of Ivan Stiefel and his team, who had multiple options for targets for their protest against mountaintop removal coal mining.

SUCCESS STORY
MOUNTAIN JUSTICE SPRING BREAK Twenty-two-
year-old **Ivan Stiefel** spearheaded the creation of an alternative spring break for university students to visit communities affected by coal industry abuses in Appalachia. In 2007, the West Virginia Mountain Justice Spring Break (MJSB) focused on securing a safe school for the children attending Marshfork Elementary, which was situated only fifty yards from a coal silo. Just beyond the silo lay a coal processing plant, a leaking coal slurry impoundment, and mountaintop removal mines.

During the Spring Break program, the West Virginia Surface Mines appeal board released a decision that would allow for a second silo to be built right next to the school. Ivan and his team decided that the governor of West Virginia had the most power to stop the construction or move the school to a new location. As such, they coordinated a peaceful sit-in at the governor's office, where dozens of activists sat down and refused to move, demanding that he build a safe new school for the children of Marshfork. The occupation ended in thirteen arrests, and although the governor made no commitments, the media attention furthered the movement for environmental justice, climate justice, and a just transition away from coal in West Virginia and beyond.

"MJSB was created to **CONNECT YOUNG PEOPLE TO THE ISSUES** of the region and then provide them a chance to **ACTIVELY JOIN THE STRUGGLE.**"
—IVAN STIEFEL

© Han Shan

So imagine you were in Ivan's shoes. You are opposing mountaintop removal mining, but against whom are you going to use a confrontational tactic? The coal company itself? The bank that invests in the coal company? The senator who continually defends the company? The governor who is allowing the silo to be built? Your choice of target could affect the type of media you garner, the way the public interprets your protest, and your success at achieving your goal.

Ivan and his team saw that the time was right—with the recent silo decision and media coverage—to target the governor. In addition, at that point the governor was a target accessible to the group. At other moments in the campaign, protests were held against Randy Huffman of the West Virginia Department of Environmental Protection; Don Blankenship, the CEO of Massey Energy; and the late U.S. Senator Robert C. Byrd. You might choose to target various individuals at different points during your efforts, all of whom have some decision-making authority.

Choosing the target may also be related to which of the entities is at the root cause of the problem—encouraging folks to look at the structures that hold environmentally destructive policies and practices in place. If you can go to the root of the issue, there's a real potential for more long-lasting change.

You may have heard other terms used in reference to protests, such as *nonviolent civil disobedience* (NVCD) or *nonviolent direct action* (NVDA). Nonviolence refers to a commitment to not engage in verbal, emotional, or physical violence toward other human beings and living creatures. Direct action refers to the use of tactics that have an immediate impact on your issue, such as blockading a logging road or the entrance to a building where a company meeting is taking place, as well as strikes, workplace occupations, and sit-ins.

Some potential goals of nonviolent direct action include:

➤ Bringing attention to an issue through mainstream media

➤ Educating the public on an issue or changing public opinion through visibility in public arenas

➤ Disrupting the status quo—the normal order of things

➤ Shutting down meetings or events

➤ Affecting those in power through their pocketbooks

➤ Shaming those who have acted irresponsibly

➤ Creating a visible show of resistance to bad policies and laws

Some actions may involve breaking a law in order to pressure a target to create political or corporate policy changes or to demonstrate that a law is unjust; this is called *civil disobedience*. An example of civil disobedience is trespassing onto private property with the intent of blockading a logging road (the actual blockading is direct action, because it's intended to actually prevent the conduct that you're protesting). Before risking arrest, particularly if you are under eighteen years of age, think very carefully about the potential financial and legal ramifications of your arrest, including the impact a police record could have on your professional and academic career in the future.

The National Lawyers Guild's (www.nlg.org) lawyers can advise you before you proceed with NVDA, to understand the potential charges and convictions you might face from this action, and can provide suggestions for finding legal observers to be on-site.

There's no magic formula for deciding which event is right for your demonstration. It may depend on the number of supporters you have, whether or not your group has a flair for the theatrical and artistic or would prefer to let professionals do the talking, and how much time you have to prepare. You can use any number of demo formats (described shortly), including marches and parades, die-ins, vigils, and general gatherings. If you've got a small crowd, you'll want to stay in one location for the duration of the demo; with one hundred-plus individuals, consider adding a moving march or parade to keep the energy high—especially if you aim to take your message to multiple targets located along a march route.

➤ A march or parade typically begins at one site, with a series of short speeches, and then moves into a leisurely walk along a prearranged route, with lots of songs, chants, posters, and banners to capture the eyes and the ears of the public.

➤ At a die-in, protesters fake their own deaths by falling or lying down in one location. Die-ins can be striking and effective protests, particularly when calling attention to the loss of human or animal life due to an environmental tragedy. Typically, individuals will lie down for a short while, five to twenty minutes, rather than occupying the space until forced to leave by campus administration or the police. Die-ins create powerful visual images for the media and the public; in addition, they can be done well with as few as twenty-five or so individuals. Although the bulk of the individuals are "dead," you'll want a few other individuals to hand out materials to passersby, plus one individual to address the crowd, explaining the purpose of the die-in.

➤ Candlelight vigils are quiet and solemn evening gatherings to commemorate disastrous events or the death or loss of freedom of individuals (such as environmental activists in Brazil jailed for opposing logging in the Amazon). You might choose to host a vigil on the sidewalk in front of the home of a corporate executive or an elected official, on your school grounds, on the sidewalk outside of a business property, or near the site of an environmental tragedy like an oil spill. Bring lots of candles and begin with a few words to frame the energy for the night and explain the issue or situation. You can invite silent time for reflection, or ask individuals to step forward to share their thoughts.

➤ Street theater (also known as guerilla theater) can be a particularly potent way to use exaggerated humor or drama to draw attention to your issue. Although lectures and speeches might turn some folks off, street theater can turn a crowd silent with awe or get them laughing hysterically. The beauty is that you don't even have to be a particularly skilled actor! Short pieces—up to five minutes—are best, with a clear message and a simple plotline. Use exaggerated speech and movements and big visual props, and don't be afraid to cause a scene—that's what you're there for.

➤ Radical cheerleading, another form of street theater, is a parody on traditional cheerleading, involving cheeky cheers with radical messages and outlandish and colorful homemade cheerleading outfits.

➤ Puppetry is a form of street theater especially useful for big actions with crowds. Larger-than-life puppets and props make a great visual for the media and help draw in a crowd. Mock funerals are another example of street theater; demonstrators mourn the loss of a person, a species, or even an idea, with a mock coffin and a funeral procession. The movie *Who Killed the Electric Car* begins with one such elaborate funeral (for the car, of course).

Choose the format that will both put pressure on your target and be achievable and fun for your group. No matter which of these demos you decide to host, I recommend getting your team trained in nonviolent direct action; The Ruckus Society (www.ruckus.org) offers trainings and referrals.

Still can't decide what kind of action to organize? Why not do them all? That's what twenty-one-year-old Sierra Crane-Murdoch, dozens of coalfield residents, and a handful of other activists chose to do when they founded Power Past Coal, a hundred-day action project that called on President Obama, the Environmental Protection Agency, and Congress to enact policies to swiftly and justly transition away from coal.

SUCCESS STORY
POWER PAST COAL Sierra Crane-Murdoch left Middlebury
College for a semester to become Power Past Coal's national coordinator. She united a diverse team of more than forty grassroots activists personally affected by the mining, processing, and burning of coal. Instead of organizing all the actions themselves, the Power Past Coal team asked groups across the country to plan actions in their own communities, generating a national upwelling of support for a transition away from coal. The team encouraged nonviolent actions of any kind—and that's what they got. Tens of thousands of citizens participated in marches, vigils, lobby

days, rallies, town hall meetings, and acts of nonviolent civil disobedience. Eventually the actions numbered over three hundred. Through it all, Sierra provided leadership, support, and media coverage to the local organizations hosting these actions.

Power Past Coal's actions were instrumental in building national pressure to move away from coal; over the course of the project, more than twenty new coal plant permits and five mountaintop removal applications were denied or suspended, while the EPA committed to regulating carbon dioxide from coal plants and coal ash from slurry ponds.

© Han Shan

"The result I'm most proud of is our engagement of **AN UNPRECEDENTED NUMBER OF CITIZENS AND LOCAL GROUPS**. Power Past Coal was proof that they're not alone in the fight." **—SIERRA CRANE-MURDOCH**

All of these actions led up to one massive mobilization, where over 2,500 citizens from Appalachia to Arizona encircled the Capitol Coal Plant in Washington, D.C., to shut down operations and risk arrest. The good news? While the protesters spoke on behalf of citizens all across the country, affected community members and others standing in solidarity had done so much work locally—through letters, media outreach, and local events in the months leading up to the protest—that they had built the public support to legitimize the protests. Even celebrities like Darryl Hannah and Martin Sheen voiced their support for the Capitol Coal Plant protest.

The planning team for the mobilization employed the following tips for a successful demo.

- ➤ Get clear on your message before you start any protest planning. Why this protest, why this target, why this location, and why now? You'll want to have a clear and concise message for the public and media that answers those questions.

- ➤ Planning a demo requires lots of tasks, including public outreach and recruitment, logistics and permits, sound and visual tech support, publicity and media outreach, legal research and support, security, chants and visuals coordination, and managing speakers. Delegate jobs in advance, and track the group's progress in each area weekly.

➤ For events drawing public attention, choose a location that sees a lot of foot traffic, or even slow car traffic. Consider obtaining permission to gather peacefully; if you're planning to march or use amplified sound like a speaker system, you may need a permit. You may have to wait weeks or months to receive a permit, so start early by contacting your city or county government. Take care of the logistics first. If you fail to get a permit for an event in advance and are denied at the last minute, you will be in a tight spot.

➤ If you decide to host an event without a permit, you may be asked by police or others to vacate the premises—be prepared and have a backup plan. To minimize that possibility, don't block entrances, sidewalks, or passages. Plan B also refers to checking the weather; what's your plan if it rains or snows, or if the heat soars to uncomfortable temperatures?

➤ It's great to have a mix of youth speakers, authorities and experts, and ordinary folks affected by your issue. A big name goes far in drawing press and attendees to your event, so shoot for the biggest celebrity you can get, even if they're famous just in your town. Let them know they'll be speaking for a short time, just three to five minutes, and that you'll have timekeepers on hand to let them know when their time is up.

➤ Invite the press, and invite them again. Select trustworthy and gregarious volunteers to greet the press and answer any questions, and prepare background materials to present to the media upon arrival. See chapter 8, Make Media Headlines, for more tips on working with the press.

➤ Spread the word! Each member of your team should personally invite at least ten people to the protest and generally spread the word to everyone they know, at school, on sports teams, in extracurricular groups, and more.

On the day of the event, make sure you've got these bases covered.

➤ If you're hosting an event with more than a handful of people, you'll want some way to amplify speakers' voices, whether it's a hand-held bullhorn or a deluxe audiovisual (AV) system. Always, always, always test any AV systems (and check bullhorns for good batteries) immediately before an event, and have a tech-savvy volunteer on hand to troubleshoot problems.

➤ If people walk by your event but don't stop to join, will they know why you're there? Yes, if you bring great visuals, like signs, banners, flags, and T-shirts that present the message unmistakably. A few members of your team can also distribute informational materials and answer questions.

➤ Think of some catchy slogans, chants, or songs that would be fitting for your event, type them up and make copies, and distribute the chant sheets at your event. Bring bullhorns to amplify the voices of the chant leaders—their energy and enthusiasm will help stir up the entire crowd. Songs can be surprisingly inspirational and appeal to a wide demographic of passersby as well, particularly if you use well-known folk songs, rock songs, or spirituals. If you are targeting a company, see whether you can adapt one of their jingles or promotional slogans with your own play on words. Good chant leaders (loud, proud, and vivacious) are key to a good protest. So grab a bullhorn and start the party.

➤ Plan the program in advance and put your most important speakers and elements first. Make sure there's an emcee that can introduce each speaker and keep the show moving by keeping speakers to their approximate times—about three minutes each. Have your most inspiring speaker close—you want to end the program on a high note! Then shift into something that will engage the crowd, like songs, chants, skits, or musical performances.

➤ There are some wild and wacky folks just waiting to show up at your public events to push their own agenda or discredit your group. If you have an open mic or other opportunities for people to publicly talk your ear off, they just might try. Prepare how to address oddball questions, long-winded statements, or the presence of the opposition, if they show.

➤ Your job's not done at the close of the event. In fact, evaluation can be one of the most important things you do. Sit down as soon as possible after the event (within a week) and look at what went well and what could be improved. Take notes to reflect on for the next event. Self-reflection is one of your group's best growth tools.

➤ Be sure to thank every volunteer who helped make the event possible, from the speakers to the logistics crew, and take time to recognize and celebrate your success before moving on to the next gig.

I mentioned earlier that visuals are key to a good protest. We're a media-hungry culture, and visual arts like film, photography, billboards, and murals speak to us in compelling ways. That's why it's critical to illustrate your cause.

Illustrate Your Cause

Using art for activism helps us quickly convey our key messages and reach a larger spectrum of the public. How? Well, your peers who don't consider themselves activists might stop to watch a play, listen to a hip-hop song, or check out a mural with an activist message—and suddenly get interested in the campaign.

Art also adds an element of fun and whimsy to gatherings that could otherwise be somewhat depressing or serious. The most celebratory and exciting activist gatherings I have witnessed have always used art as a central component for education and outreach. Providing a visual centerpiece for your work can also help you snag a photo and caption in the local newspaper or a short feature on local television news, drawing even more attention to your campaign.

Try to appeal to people's eyes and ears. Whenever possible, appeal to their hands, too—give them something physical to do or hold at the event. Here are some ways to reach people's eyes, ears, and hands.

➤ A sea of banners or signs with the same message, colors, and font presents the image of a unified movement. Bold letters and short, punchy phrases work best. In this case, the fewer the words, the better. Make sure your signs can be read from afar: fifty feet or more is a good gauge. If possible, bring enough signs to hand out to a number of the individuals who show up—it gives people a sense of purpose, which can keep them around longer!

➤ You can march with banners, hold them up outside stores and offices, and drape or hang them over the sides of buildings. Cloth banners take longer to make, but can be used repeatedly; banners on giant pieces of paper are best for a one-time use. If you're making a cloth banner, choose a timeless message you can use over and over again. Give the job of holding a banner to supporters who show up. Hold banners taut if you want to snag a top-notch photo—newspaper photographers won't be interested in a droopy banner.

➤ Flyers are a key tool in any activist's tool kit. To make interesting, eye-catching flyers, stick to using just a few fonts, and use varying sizes, styles, borders, and other elements to break up text. An image should be central to your flyer—people are more attracted to images than to text. So keep your text minimal: the essential who, what, when, where, and why. Print your flyer on brightly colored paper. The same old black and white is boring, and it won't stand out to people passing by a message board.

Although all of these demo planning tips and action visuals are important, remember the core of the success of a demo: building public support, exhausting other options to persuade the decision maker, and choosing a strategic date, location, and target.

A word of warning: even when your protest is smart, strategic, and part of an escalating series of tactics designed to create real environmental change, you may encounter critics who label you a troublemaker. If that happens, you won't be the first change-maker to be called a troublemaker—think about Gandhi's role in the movement for independence in India, the American colonists dumping tea into Boston harbor as a form of protest against high taxes imposed by England, and Rosa Parks refusing to move from her seat for a white passenger during the Montgomery Bus Boycott. She was kicked off the bus, but by taking a stand she helped incite the civil rights movement to victory. If you find yourself labeled a troublemaker, you are in good company.

NEXT STOP: MAKE MEDIA HEADLINES

No protest should be planned without a media outreach strategy. You might reach a hundred attendees at your demonstration. If the press comes, your audience could be ten thousand readers—that's a hundred times larger. In fact, for any action plan, the media is one of your best tools to spread your message on a large scale, particularly when operating on a shoestring budget. Need funds? Send out a press release detailing your recent victories and your next ambition, and inviting folks to contribute. Want to pressure your decision maker for an upcoming vote? Consider targeting that person in a letter to the editor. Think the environmental practices of a particular company stink? Use your own media skills to blog and create short videos about their impact. The next chapter will teach you how to leverage the media for your cause.

RESOURCES

National Lawyers Guild, www.nlg.org The National Lawyers Guild's members—lawyers, law students, jailhouse lawyers, and legal workers united in chapters and committees—can offer support and advice to protesters before, during, and after actions.

Organizing for Power, Organizing for Change, www.organizingfor power.wordpress.com Organizing for Power is a compilation of resources, including nonviolent strategies and tactics, from more than thirty-five years of grassroots organizing.

Ruckus Society, www.ruckus.org The Ruckus Society provides environmental, human rights, and social justice organizers with the tools, training, and support needed to achieve their goals, particularly in the realm of NVDA. On their website you'll find manuals on subjects like planning nonviolent direct actions and creating action visuals (like banners).

08
MAKE MEDIA
HEADLINES

USE TRADITIONAL AND
NEW MEDIA FOR PUBLICITY

I n the spring of 2007, a few friends fresh out of Middlebury College turned a simple idea into one of the largest and most pivotal climate change demonstrations ever seen. Jon Warnow and May Boeve joined four friends and their professor Bill McKibben to launch a group called "Step It Up 2007." Their demand—for Congress to commit the United States to an 80 percent reduction in carbon emissions by 2050—was based on sound science backed by the Intergovernmental Panel on Climate Change (IPCC), the organization founded by the United Nations Environment Programme that shared the 2007 Nobel Peace Prize with Al Gore.

The Step It Up 2007 team called for a National Day of Climate Action that would capture the attention and spark the imagination of the media, public, and politicians. They organized the event by sending emails and making calls to friends and organizations across the nation. The team encouraged creative actions with compelling visual elements, and asked each group to capture their event on camera and upload the shots online. They didn't want people hopping in their cars or flying in airplanes, spewing carbon on their way across the country to a march in Washington, D.C.

So instead they asked people to gather for events locally with fellow community members.

Just three months later, the day of action was a smashing success, involving more than 1,400 communities in all fifty states. Nearly every event captured photos of posters and banners with the same call to action: "Congress, Cut Carbon 80% by 2050." Step It Up 2007 was incredibly effective at nationwide online organizing—everything was coordinated or distributed through the website, including event registration, fun videos, action maps, organizing tools, and a massive interactive photo exhibit. The use of the Internet as the central hub for the campaign tied many dispersed actions together and made it into a national story, ripe for grabbing the media's attention.

It worked. Instead of reaching just the tens of thousands of individuals who would have witnessed or participated in a community action, Step It Up 2007's media success brought the climate crisis to the attention of millions of individuals. The message reached hundreds of press outlets, including *Good Morning America, USA Today*, and the *New York Times*, all of which reported on the urgency of the climate crisis and the rise of a citizen movement that was turning up the pressure on politicians.

Soon after, the top three Democratic contenders in the 2008 presidential race—including then-Senator Barack Obama—began calling for 80-percent carbon reductions by 2050. By the end of the year, Step It Up 2007 had changed the political landscape by moving what had been a radical idea into a mainstream and popular political platform. Essential to the success was not only the mobilization of tens of thousands of individuals who participated in a community event but also the effective use of the media to reach an audience of tens of millions.

Like the organizers of Step It Up, you have a choice. You can tell your story one room at a time, to fifty or so people. Or, you can generate media attention and communicate to five thousand, or five hundred thousand, or five million people! So how do you get your message out to an audience of policy makers, allies, decision makers, educators, and administrators? It all starts with a good story about your campaign—a story that will live beyond an individual event or press release. Then it's about spreading the story. You have two options: you can create and distribute your own media (by blogging, social networking, making videos, and building a website) and you can reach out to the traditional media to tell your story.

CRAFTING YOUR STORY AND CHOOSING YOUR AUDIENCE

What's more impressive and unique: a fifteen-year-old raising $10,000 to restore her local watershed, or an adult doing the same? The former, of course—and that's the story likely to snag a news reporter's attention. When it comes to traditional media outlets, your age can work to your advantage, and you can attract media interest more easily than the average adult. However, although your precocious activities may capture attention initially, you want to draw the audience in with your message. Before you can pitch a story or share it with reporters, you need to frame your story and choose your audience.

Frame Your Story

Framing means looking at the entire mural of your campaign or issue and deciding which section you want to share with the world. In creating a frame, you deliberately leave some things out in order to highlight other things. For example, if you are trying to shut down a polluting chemical refinery, you can tell a number of different stories: will you focus on the water pollution frame, the air pollution frame, or the frame of corrupt local officials in collusion with the refinery executives? Framing is about developing the conversation you want the public to engage in. Environmental activists are sometimes disregarded because it seems that they care more about animals or landscapes than humans. Part of framing your story is presenting it in a way that has the potential to resonate with people who don't consider themselves to be environmentalists.

Know Your Audience

No matter what issue you are working on, knowing how to work with the media can help you achieve your goals, but only if you have a plan. First, you need to know your audience. Who are you trying to influence? Are you trying to get your city council to put up solar panels on government buildings? Do you want to raise money to support wildlife conservation efforts for migrating birds? Do you want to encourage local high school students to start recycling efforts?

In each case, you are trying to reach a different group of people. As you start to ask these questions, the media outlets you want to spend your time reaching out to become apparent. For each campaign, you will have a different audience and you can focus on talking to a reporter at the metro section of the local newspaper, a national birders' magazine, or local high school newspapers. Reporters get press releases unrelated to their interests all the time; by narrowing your focus you will stand out and find the outlets that really want to tell your story.

Craft Your Message

Once you decide what message will best resonate, and your ideal audience, the following four tips—know your stuff, stand out, make it personal, and make it timely—will help you craft a newsworthy story angle.

TIP 1: KNOW YOUR STUFF.

Journalists want to hear your perspective; they are always on the lookout for a fresh new take on an old issue or a heads-up on emerging issues. But how many of them have time to research every relevant political, environmental, and social issue on a daily basis? Win their trust by demonstrating mastery of facts and figures and presenting your information in a compelling and unbiased way. If you bring carefully researched, well-reasoned arguments to their attention, you're doing them a favor.

If you are part of an organization, pitch your issue or the individuals at the heart of the organization, not the organization itself. Journalists are wary of doing stories that appear to be biased public relations stories for organizations, even if they agree with the organization's perspective. Keep in mind that journalists are under pressure to produce balanced stories and will often contact the organization or individuals that represent the "opposite" side of your story.

TIP 2: STAND OUT.

Think like reporters. They may love your story, but when their editors ask why the story matters, what will the reporters say?

Superlatives: Articulate what's unique about your organization and its approach. Is your project the first of its kind in your city? The biggest in the state? Are you hosting the largest student gathering your city has ever seen? Are you the youngest person to ever pass a city resolution in Wichita, Kansas? Are you the youngest constituents of a statewide coalition pushing for water quality legislation? Think first, biggest, youngest, and largest: reporters love superlatives!

Controversy: Spotlight any conflict inherent in your campaign. David and Goliath-style stories, in which an underdog goes to battle against a big, powerful figure or institution, can capture the interest and sympathy of a reporter—and the public.

TIP 3: MAKE IT PERSONAL.

People love reading about other people. Fess up: when's the last time you peeked at a celebrity gossip magazine? You need to make your story personal. Pitch the people involved in the campaign, first and foremost, as a window into the issue. You can also invite someone famous or a well-known local figure to support the campaign, give a media quote, or put that recognizable name in the press release headline.

Major population areas will often have culture-specific publications. Does your issue strongly affect one cultural or ethnic group? For example, if you're trying to expand green space in a predominantly Korean-American neighborhood, do outreach to the Korean-American newspaper in town.

TIP 4: MAKE IT TIMELY.

There are lots of time-sensitive "handles" for media releases: a new campaign, an upcoming vote, a campaign victory such as passage of a bill or an adoption of a new policy, a public event like a toxic tour or community fair, a protest, the anniversary of a historical event (such as the *Exxon Valdez* spill) linked to your campaign, release of a new report or new information, or the announcement of a new coalition member or influential individual lending support to your work. Make the case for why your story is relevant now.

GETTING YOUR STORY HEARD FAR AND WIDE

Now that you know what story to share with traditional media outlets, how can you catch the media's attention? First, try to find a mentor in the business: local reporters might be willing to introduce you to the local media landscape. Take them out to lunch, pick their brains, and build a long-term relationship, so you can test future story ideas or get referrals for other outlets. Whether or not a mentor assists you along the way, these five steps will help you get your story heard far and wide: build your media list, prepare your materials, pitch the story, prepare for the interview, and debrief.

Build Your Media List

Every group should have a media list on hand. You have a few options: build it yourself, share it, or buy it. Creating a media list from scratch can take a lot of time and energy. So try to get a list from a local nonprofit (like a local Sierra Club chapter, for example) or a public agency like the mayor's office or county school board. Sometimes all it takes is a web search and a few simple calls—you might be surprised how willing people are to help. Reach out and ask them to support your group by sharing their list. If you're working with a local company, see whether their media team will share their list and offer media support.

Buying lists is costly—I wouldn't recommend it. Media services like Green Media Toolshed or Cision are sometimes available for free at your local library or social justice resource center. These services provide access to a regularly updated database of reporters across the nation, and they provide tools to expedite sending out media releases.

To build your own list, look for the following outlets: television and radio stations, magazines, daily and weekly newspapers, and websites (particularly blogs and youth-driven content sites). Most of the contact information can be found in the phone book or on the outlet's website. For each contact, capture their name, official title, focus area or interests, name of outlet, address, email, phone, and fax. Some reporters may love emails and hate faxes, or prefer you call them directly with pitches. Ask how they prefer to be reached—and honor their request. To ensure a better response, send the press release to the attention of the environmental reporter or special interest reporter and use their name and personal email or direct fax.

LETTERS TO THE EDITOR AND OTHER OPINION PIECES

Most newspapers invite letters to the editor and opinion pieces. Letters to the editor are short, usually under 300 words, and should address a recent article or an issue raised in the paper. Did you read about plans for the expansion of a waste dump? Use that opportunity to write a letter to the editor about the financial and environmental benefits of increased recycling programs in the community. Guest opinion pieces are longer—but often no more than 750 or so words—and may cover anything from opinions on local environmental issues to issues hot on the national scale. Check out the requirements for submission on your paper's webpage or on the opinion page.

TV and radio producers love youth stories: youth helping other youth, youth taking an unpopular but principled stand, youth helping the environment, youth helping animals. Use this to your advantage! Check your local television listings to see who is actually in your area, because many local TV stations are happy to cover any event that gets them out of the studio and covering a visually exciting story.

Brainstorm a list of magazines that cover your issue. Think *Outside* if you're working on wilderness conservation, or *Yes!* magazine for community-based sustainability initiatives. Do the same for publications that target your age demographic, like *New York Times Upfront* or *Seventeen*. These magazines look for stories up to a year in advance; don't think you can pitch them one day and see your story coming out a month or two later. Typically they need a lead time of a minimum of six months, often more. Many magazines are now launching annual green issues (sometimes around Earth Day, but not always) and again, the stories of the people behind the issue are often just as important as the issue itself. To make the cut for the Earth Day issue, pitch your story no later than early fall of the prior year.

Search for the "assignment desk," "news desk," or "city desk" contact at every newspaper outlet in your region. In the past newspapers tended to have specific "beat" reporters who would cover specific stories, like science and technology, education, or health care. Due to changes in the newspaper industry, reporters now tend to wear many hats, but it doesn't hurt to inquire about specific beats.

Use Google Blog Search or Technorati (www.technorati.com) to search for blogs that cover your issue. Pitch their writers on your story or ask whether you can submit your own blog post. Brower Youth Award alumni regularly post to prominent blogs like the Huffington Post (www.huffington post.com), Grist Magazine (www.grist.org), and It's Getting Hot in Here (www.itsgettinghotinhere.org). Other websites that spotlight youth-created writing, blogs, and stories include TakingITGlobal (www.tigweb.org), Youth Noise (www.youthnoise.com), and Campus Progress (www.campus progress.org).

Prep Your Materials

Key media materials include press releases, press advisories, and press kits. A press release is a one-page news story, written in the third person, about a group, a person, an event, or a campaign. Advisories are much shorter than releases: they include the who, what, when, where, and why in clear and brief terms and are sent in advance of an event to invite the media to attend. A press kit is a more exhaustive backgrounder that you present to the media when they arrive at your event.

Press releases (also called news releases) can cover events, but they also can serve to announce your group's response to a political vote, a statement by your decision maker, the release of a new report, or anything else that doesn't involve an on-the-ground event. In the one-page release, your job is to pique the reporter's interest. If a reporter bites, she will likely follow up with an interview before finalizing the story.

The press release should present the most important information in the first paragraph. Each paragraph should be three or four sentences, ideally. Include at least one statement in quotes from a credible spokesperson in the second or third paragraph. The last paragraph includes more background information about your group and the issue.

Reporters often lift language word-for-word out of your release. Use this to your advantage, to brand the kind of language you want the media (and the public) to use in reference to your group or your issue. If you want to be known as the "the most effective youth environmental lobbying group in Connecticut," use that language in the release. Just make sure it's an accurate representation—you could lose your credibility if you exaggerate!

Put some time and thought into the title and subtitle of your press release, as well as the subject line for emails: as the first thing a reporter sees, these need to capture their attention quickly. On emails, DON'T CAPITALIZE YOUR SUBJECT LINE, OR USE WACKY FORMATTING!!! Don't you find that sort of stuff annoying? Reporters will, too.

If you would like to invite the press to an event, start outreach one to two weeks in advance with a press advisory. Keep in mind that, unlike a press release, this advisory just covers the details of the event: who, what, when, where, and why. Advance notice is important for smaller outlets that may have only one roving photographer or a camera crew that needs to schedule travel with advance notice—follow up again a few days before the event. Bigger outlets, however, typically make their decisions only on that day. Although you should send the advisory two or three days before the event, be sure to send it again that morning so it's sitting on their desks when they make their early morning decisions about what events to attend that day.

Press kits can include an overview of your group and mission, photos and profiles of key group members, a list of any victories or projects undertaken to date, one to three recent news releases, and key past news clips. It's often useful to include detailed fact sheets, frequently asked questions, or the summaries from government or university reports—anything that bolsters your arguments. Put together digital and print versions of your press kit, to email or hand out in person during your events. Assign a media liaison to meet up with the reporter, hand out the press kit and, most important, gather business cards or contact information of any attending reporters so you can follow up. Be sure to ask when they expect the story to be printed.

Pitch It and Follow Through

Send out your releases via fax or email. Particularly if your news is time-sensitive, send the release early in the news cycle—just before 9 A.M. local time. Wait a half hour or so and start following up via phone.

Follow-through makes the difference between all of those releases going into the trash and ensuring that your issue gets coverage. News desks get hundreds of faxes and emails daily. A catchy title and subtitle might get you a second look, but follow-up phone calls are key. When you call, if you don't have a particular contact in mind, ask for the assignment editor.

Master the fifteen-second pitch: your opening line needs to capture the reporter's interest. A communications professional once said that he pitched a story on ocean pollution like this: "Have you ever had a mercury sandwich?" Reporters would pause and try to figure out his meaning, or chuckle, giving him an opening to dive into the problem of mercury pollution making its way into fish—and ultimately into our bodies. Isn't that a more creative pitch than "Did you know that excessive mercury pollution in the world's oceans poses a grave human health concern?"

Always make personal contact. Phone is best (leave a message if you can't get through to a live person), and a follow-up email is next best. Reporters constantly ask me to fax or email a news release I had sent only an hour before—saying they missed it on the first round. Sometimes those phone calls turn into stories—and sometimes, big stories! So don't be afraid to call. Newspaper and television journalists can be gruff, and often they're working under a deadline. Calling early in the morning (before 10:30 A.M.) is helpful—stories are just being assigned for the day, and it's unlikely that reporters are already under a time crunch to submit the day's pieces.

Make extra sure that your contact information listed on your outreach materials is accurate and that your phone and email are checked regularly. You do not want a reporter calling or emailing at the last minute and not reaching you. You might not get another chance.

Prepare for the Interview

Choose your core message. The average television sound bite is ten seconds or less; the print average is five to twenty-five words. Only a few sentences will ultimately make the cut, so make sure you repeat your core messages again and again.

Practice! Think of all the questions a reporter may pose and draft your ideal answers. Practice those answers in mock interviews until you're confident that you can communicate your core ideas confidently and succinctly.

Research the outlet. What types of stories do they run? Read the news, watch a television show, or listen to a radio show before your appearance. Know who listens to, reads, or watches their coverage, and prepare to reach

TIPS FOR TV INTERVIEWS

Keep still. Gesticulating wildly or moving your body around just distracts the audience from your cause. If you're going on TV, see whether you can do some practice recordings (even with a friend's cell phone or digital camera) to see how you perform under pressure.

Dress to impress. Wear clothes in a single color (but no dark blue or black), and dress as professionally as possible. Don't let a sloppy appearance get in the way of your message.

It's okay if you mess up, but be professional. If you're not doing a live show, wave your hand in front of your face if you mess up. They won't use it. Let them know if you don't feel comfortable at any point. You don't have to finish a thought if you stumble—you can just start over. However, if it's live, keep your cool. Breathe, slow down, and get back on track as quickly as possible. Mistakes feel a hundred times worse than they look; they usually aren't even noticed by viewers unless you react in a way that shows you messed up.

that audience. Find out what kind of a story the outlet is doing: length, what angle, live or not, topics for discussion, when it will air, who else will be interviewed, and more.

If someone approaches you out of the blue, research the reporter and the outlet. You don't want to be put in the hot seat unexpectedly! I heard about a colleague in the environmental movement who was invited to appear on a television talk show. It turned out the show wasn't a legitimate talk show— it was actually a satirical TV series starring British comedian Sacha Baron Cohen and featuring the character Ali G. Do your homework.

Learn how to bridge. *Bridging* is redirecting the conversation back to your core message. Have you noticed how politicians are experts at this? They never answer a question if they don't want to—they simply take the conversation in a new direction. Although this can be frustrating for the journalist, it ensures that you are in the driver's seat for the interview.

The ABCs of bridging are A: *Acknowledge* the question and B: *Bridge* back to your C: *Content.* For example, you're at a protest doing a media interview when the TV journalist asks you how your parents feel about your activism. Are you sure you want your five to thirteen seconds of fame

TIPS FOR RADIO INTERVIEWS

Find a quiet place where you can guarantee you won't be interrupted for the course of the interview. Also make sure you won't have any phones ringing, call-waiting beeps, or other disturbances. Landlines typically have better sound quality for interviews than cell phones. If you're worried about noise and the radio station is local, see whether you can go in for the interview. It's also more fun in person!

Keep hydrated. Have water on hand while being interviewed—you don't want to be distracted by a dry mouth.

Make it a conversation. There's another person on the line interviewing you. Be personable! If you are face-to-face with your interviewer, you will probably sound more conversational—another great reason to do the interview in person, if possible. Thank them for having you on the show, crack jokes (if you are confident they'll go over well), relax, engage in a fluid conversation, and thank the host again at the end of the interview for inviting you to share your perspective.

If they can't see you, cheat! It's okay to have your key talking points written down in front of you, but don't sound like you are reading. You can also ask a reporter to call back at a certain time while you prepare for the interview. Unless the reporter has a pending deadline, you can ask for a call back if you need time to get ready.

to focus on what your parents think? Maybe you'd prefer to snag a sound bite about the issue and your campaign. You can quickly acknowledge the question and head straight into your key message: "My parents are thrilled that I have a strong voice. I'm using that voice to put pressure on American auto companies to create more fuel-efficient cars. The time for gas-guzzling SUVs is past, and American consumers want eco-friendly transportation options." Once you capture the reporter's attention, you need to help direct the story and make sure your key points get out.

Prepare backgrounders. Bring background materials, like a press kit, to share with the reporter, or email them background materials after the interview.

Clueless? You can say, "I don't know the answer to that. But what I do know is . . ." and lead into a fact supporting your cause. Don't ever say "no comment." And don't ever fabricate an answer, or guess, if you don't have the facts. One untruth can haunt you—and your group—until the end of time.

Debrief and Share the Piece

Read the articles, listen to the radio interviews, and watch the television clips. Debrief the coverage with your group—what went well? Did your spokesperson stay on message? In what direction did the reporter take the story? Are you happy with the coverage? If there are any mistakes, ask the media outlet to publish a correction. If you are happy with the coverage, it's a great idea to send a note to the reporter with a thank-you for the coverage.

Get copies of all articles and find the links to online radio or television clips. Keep your originals in a folder in one place, both in hardcopy and online. You'll want to share these, and it's hard to track them down months after the fact. Send a note or a copy of the piece around to anyone who might be interested: potential donors, your target, friends and family, and of course your campaign's financial supporters. Include a sidebar on your blog or website with links to online media articles.

NEW MEDIA

When I started environmental campaigning, the media landscape was dominated by fifty or so firms. Fewer than a dozen giant companies—among them Time Warner, Disney, Rupert Murdoch's News Corporation, and Sony—dominated the film, television, book, magazine, and music production and publication industries. If you couldn't appeal to the bigwigs, there were limited opportunities to get your story out. Nowadays, daily newspapers and traditional media outlets are falling like dominoes and more and more folks are finding their news (and even new friends and dates) online.

The good news? That makes it easier for us to get our stories out without an intermediary. Online platforms for media creation now offer you the tools to launch your own web-based show, website, podcast, radio station, or blog.

Why should you tap into the new media craze? Well, for starters, the average American teen is spending about three hours per day online—as much time as they spend watching television. Even American adults are spending more than a dozen hours weekly surfing the Internet, and more than half log on daily. The Web is where the public is, and if you want to capture their attention, it's time to get savvy with these web-based tools. Not only that, but the best communication is word of mouth, and social networking is the twenty-first-century version of word of mouth with a huge potential for a positive ripple effect.

The rest of this chapter guides you through some of the best tools to get your story out without relying on the traditional media.

Blogging

What makes a blog great? Well, you do! You should bring your unique perspective and fresh take on environmental challenges and solutions. Thousands of new blogs come into the world daily, but few garner an audience of more than a few hundred people.

You can launch your own blog as a solo enterprise, if you have time to maintain it regularly and aggressively recruit an audience. However, I'd recommend getting your start by posting on existing environmental and political blogrolls mentioned earlier, like The Huffington Post, It's Getting Hot in Here, and Grist Magazine. You won't have to worry about driving traffic to your blog, because each of these sites already draws big crowds. Instead, you can focus your time on writing great content and spreading the word to your personal networks. If and when the time comes for you to go solo, you will have a better understanding of the blogging world and will have built a name for yourself as a blogger.

A good blog entry starts with an eye-catching and informative title, like "Why We Fight" or "Young, Green, and Out of Work"—titles chosen by BYA recipient Billy Parish for the climate change youth blog It's Getting Hot in Here. Titles get scanned by search engines like Google, so if you want your blog to come up in Google searches on a particular issue, choose relevant keywords. Then follow up with great content: publicize a little-known news story with your own spin, tell your personal story of organizing in your community, or use your blog post as an opportunity to praise (or criticize) the actions of key political and environmental leaders. Whatever you do, put your own voice and perspective into the blog: don't simply repeat news you've just found elsewhere.

Blogs, by nature, are personal, so tell your readers who you are. In your profile section, share a few tidbits about your personal and environmental interests and your background, and consider adding a photo. Example: "Elissa is currently living in Ottawa, where she spends far too much time daydreaming about camping and skiing instead of working! For the past few years Elissa has been actively seeking to strengthen the youth environmental movement and increase youth participation in decision making."

If you want to launch your own blog, Blogger and Wordpress are easy-to-use sites. Making your blog a success requires a few things: a great launch, a growing audience, and your capacity to add new content weekly and interact with your readers. Start with at least three interesting blog posts; otherwise, your blog will look skeletal. Every time people visit your blog, they'll have the opportunity to flag it for a return. Give them enough juicy content on their first visit to ensure a return visit, and make it easy by including a link to your RSS feeds, which are tools that help subscribers get an update each time you post a new blog entry. Place this RSS button near the top of the page, in the part of the web page that is visible without scrolling.

It's Getting Hot in Here is an example of young people working together to build a community and audience bigger than what any one student or youth leader could expect on an individual blog site. By working together, almost three hundred leaders tell stories from all over the United States and collectively reach thousands of readers daily. Look for collaborative opportunities like It's Getting Hot in Here to tell your story through outlets that exist to help you!

Twitter

Using Twitter, a microblogging service, is a super-easy way to send campaign updates. A *tweet* is a post or status update of 140 characters or less—short and sweet. Twitter is particularly useful for big events or time-sensitive email or phone campaigns. You can let people know your protest has been cancelled or moved to a new location, just by sending a quick Tweet to your "followers."

Sign up for a Twitter account for your organization; create a short profile; link to any other social networking sites, blogs, or websites; and upload a logo or picture. Then send out a note to your networks asking them to sign up as "followers." They can decide how they want to hear from you—via the Web, instant messaging, or text. Use microblogging as a way to keep your issue on people's minds. If you have interesting, funny, or thoughtful posts, readers are more likely to follow you and stay involved in your work.

Twitter really shines for rapid-response situations and breaking news. Did a politician promise something at your rally that you weren't expecting? Using Twitter, you can tell the world. Reporters, bloggers, and political campaigns are always tracking Twitter for news. Be the first to make an announcement, and you might become the source for the next big article. If you can get many individuals at a conference or a protest tweeting about what they are seeing and doing, a small turnout on the ground could turn out to have a greatly amplified impact and be seen by folks nationally and even globally.

Social Networking Sites

You probably belong to a number of social networking sites like Facebook and MySpace, which feature user-generated content, personal profiles, friend networks, and more. In terms of the number of registered users, if Facebook were a nation, it would be one of the largest countries in the world! Although you may have your personal profile page and friends, have you launched a page to publicize your campaign and recruit supporters?

Use social networking sites to spread the word about upcoming events, recruit new volunteers, raise money, and educate more folks about your issue, with a few clicks of the mouse. Each time your supporters announce they're attending one of your events, become a fan of your group, or post on your profile, each of their friends gets word. Imagine: they're doing free advertising for you!

It's easy enough to start a page; the real value in these sites develops when you start growing the community of supporters. Your page needs to be updated regularly with new posts and content, and you should do regular basic maintenance, like approving friends and answering mail. Making "friends" should be one of your biggest priorities, especially at first. Email your friends and colleagues with instructions on how to friend you, and include a template they can forward to invite their own friends. Thank each new friend by posting a quick message on his or her wall. Especially when you first launch, make sure you hop online daily to respond to inquiries— you want to take advantage of the buzz of your launch.

What else can you do with your sites? Post songs, a quiz or survey, or videos and photographs from your campaign; write blog entries; and send messages to individual supporters or the entire group. When you've got a birthday coming up, post a status update asking people to donate to your cause or your group instead of giving a present. Check out tutorials on the individual social networking sites for more tips on how to use them successfully.

Videos and Podcasting

You can use the power of video to open the world's eyes to the environmental crises we're facing. Okay, so maybe your viral video won't be watched millions of times, like Annie Leonard's twenty-minute *Story of Stuff* video (a must-see!). But by posting on YouTube, Facebook, and MySpace and promoting using social networking tools, you can help spread the word to an audience of hundreds or thousands.

With so many of us constantly plugged into our portable media players these days, podcasting is another sure way to reach a population on the move. Podcasts are series of audio or video files that you can listen to (or watch) online or download to take on the go. The best podcasts are typically short pieces (five to ten minutes) and offer an interview of a specialist on an issue, short news stories, or reflections on a campaign. Subscribers are alerted each time a new podcast is available and can listen to it wherever and whenever they want.

Check out the "Brower Youth Awards" video podcast at the iTunes store, under the podcast section—it's free!

NEXT STOP: GROW THE GREEN

You never know what doors even one media article can open for you. Beyond public education and influencing your target, a great reason to make media headlines is that media coverage can attract resources to your campaign— like financial donations, volunteers, or pro bono support from professionals willing to loan their expertise. A favorable article can also establish your credibility to potential donors and supporters. Need more ideas on how to raise funds for your campaign? Keep reading—the next chapter details the best funding sources for youth organizing.

RESOURCES

Campus Progress, www.campusprogress.org Campus Progress's journalism program provides funding, training, and editorial guidance to a diverse network of print, online, and broadcast media on college campuses across the country.

Center for Media Justice, www.centerformediajustice.org The Center for Media Justice is a media strategy and action center that uses strategic communications and media activism to support social change, focused on everything from building relationships with journalists to creating great press events.

Don't Think of an Elephant!: Know Your Values and Frame the Debate—The Essential Guide for Progressives, by George Lakoff. White River Junction, VT: Chelsea Green, 2004.

Fired Up Media, www.firedupmedia.com Fired Up Media is an award-winning network and training organization for videographers, photographers, bloggers, and journalists reporting from the front lines of the youth climate movement.

Listen Up!, www.listenup.org Listen Up! is a youth media network that connects young video producers and their allies to resources, support, and projects to achieve an authentic youth voice in the mass media.

New Organizing Institute (NOI), www.neworganizing.com NOI works to train and support a new generation of technology-enabled campaigners, focused on cutting-edge online organizing techniques like writing effective emails, engaging bloggers, leveraging social networks, and using video.

SPIN Project, www.spinproject.org The SPIN Project provides accessible and affordable strategic communications consulting, training, coaching, networking opportunities, and concrete tools.

Step It Up 2007, www.stepitup2007.org See how this team, led in part by Brower Youth Award recipients, coordinated one of the largest days of action on climate change, while using new and traditional media to broadcast their message far and wide.

09
GROW THE GREEN

HOW TO ASK FOR (AND GET!) FINANCIAL SUPPORT

t's no secret that the people who have the most money often call the shots in our world. By learning to raise and manage funds successfully, you can ensure that financial resources are being directed toward the creation of a just, green world rather than toward its destruction. Most environmental projects, events, and campaigns require at least some funding, which makes fundraising a critical aspect of every group's work. Plus, asking people to align their money with their values is a great way to build a movement of committed supporters. Individuals are more invested in projects to which they give their money, time, and resources, even when their contributions are relatively small.

Becoming a great fundraiser is a terrific personal asset, too. If you want to run your own business or head up a nonprofit in the future, strong fundraising skills are essential. One of the key roles of nonprofit executive directors is to fundraise and ensure the financial sustainability of their organization. To launch a for-profit business, unless you have enough cash to provide all of the seed capital yourself, you will most likely need to seek a loan or investment from a bank or wealthy individuals. Learning how to make a compelling case for your passions and asking for financial support will help you in many ways down the road.

And getting comfortable with fundraising for your cause will help you develop the confidence to seek financial support—like fellowships, grants, scholarships, and loans—to pursue all of your passions. With the right fundraising skills, you can even create your own dream job.

FUNDRAISING MADE EASY

So is there any silver bullet—a quick and easy way to raise money? Yes, actually, there is: you can ask an individual to give a donation. Contrary to what you might expect, most philanthropic giving doesn't come from companies, the government, or big foundations. Each year, only about 25 percent of nonprofit funds are generated from these sources. The other 75 percent of nonprofit funds comes from individuals. And not just wealthy individuals! Seven out of ten adults donate money, and most of these people, are not rich. These are people like your parents, the parents of your friends, your coworkers and your supervisors at work, or your sports coach.

Think about it: have you ever given money to someone you know? Maybe your friend is running a marathon to raise money for cancer research, or your next-door neighbor is selling cookies or chocolates to fund his or her sports team. Whether your donation was $5 or $50, you probably felt good about helping them reach their goals. That's why it's a great idea to start your fundraising campaign by asking everyone you know for a donation.

Okay, so asking for money might not be your favorite thing to do. You're not alone. A lot of people dread fundraising because they feel guilty about asking people for money or they are afraid of rejection. As activists, we might avoid fundraising roles or try fundraisers that don't require us to actually ask for money. This cycle of beliefs, feelings, and behaviors is normal, but it's incredibly debilitating if you're trying to raise money for your great nonprofit cause! A big part of being an effective fundraiser, or contributing to fundraising, is wrestling with your own deep-seated fears about asking people for money. If you want money, you have to ask for it.

What's the worst that can happen if you ask for money? Someone will say no. That's not so bad. People say no for all sorts of reasons, many of which you can't control: maybe they have unexpected medical bills that month, or they just gave a contribution to another group, or their child is attending a pricey college. On the other hand, the best that can happen is that someone will say yes.

Remember the law of halves from chapter 3? Fundraising experts estimate that about half of the people you personally ask for a donation will give; the other half will say no. Of the folks who say yes, about half will give you what you ask for; the other half will give less than the amount you ask for. Those are pretty good odds. (People will rarely give you more than you ask for.)

So let's get started! The best way to ask people for money is to ask them face-to-face. Here's a how-to guide.

Making the Ask: Who?

First, ask your family. They love you the most, so you can make the hardest sell. Then ask your friends. They also love you, and you support them when they need it, too. Next, ask your neighbors; they know you well, and giving locally is neighborly. If you have coworkers, ask them for support. When you've spoken to everyone in these categories, reach out to your networks—groups, clubs, organizations, or cohorts that you (or your parents) belong to—like your church, your local hiking club, your sports team, and your school's PTA association. Remember, people who know you are most likely to become donors, even if they don't have a large income. Finally, when you've exhausted your personal networks, go to other community organizations, businesses, and service groups, such as green businesses, local unions, and Kiwanis, Lions, and Rotary clubs.

Making the Ask: Where?

If you are targeting groups, ask to get on the agenda at their next meeting, so you can present your fundraising pitch to the entire group.

If you are targeting an individual, make a personal visit to her home or work or take her out to a meal or coffee. Most people don't like to be surprised with a fundraising request, so it's absolutely fine to ask someone in advance if you can meet with her to tell her more about your work and ask for her financial support. If a meeting is out of the question, call her. Resist the urge to leave a phone message or send an email or a letter outlining your financial ask. Those may seem like easier, less scary, or more fun options, but they are much less effective—people can easily ignore your request.

Making the Ask: How?

When you are targeting a group, set a fundraising goal. People like to feel like they're part of a collective action that will be more effective than their individual actions, and this includes giving money. If you give $20 to a cause, you may feel like that's only a drop in the bucket. However, if you join forty-nine other people each giving $20, that becomes $1,000—a sum that has more impact.

Make it easy for people to give. If you are at a meeting of the group, provide pens for people to write checks, a gift form in which donors fill out their contact information and check a box indicating the amount they're giving, and envelopes for cash and checks. If possible, have a friend or member of your team pass out the materials while you're giving your pitch, or place the materials on everyone's chair or table before the meeting starts. (Of course, you'll want to ask permission to do this before the meeting begins.) If your group has 501(c)(3) status, be sure to let people know—this means their donations are tax-deductible. Provide a receipt to each donor in the form of a thank-you letter.

Begin your pitch by introducing yourself and thanking the group members for their time. Then give your elevator pitch (see page 56). If you have only a few minutes to talk, save at least the second half of your presentation for your ask. Here's an example of one way to go about asking for support:

"I've told you a bit about our work and our goal of helping ten small-business owners, serving more than 25,000 customers in our town, to become certified green businesses in the next eighteen months. Big numbers like this deserve big support! So tonight I have a favor to ask of you all. To help make our city one of the greenest in the state, we need your financial assistance. If we can raise $1,000 tonight from this group, we can offer five free workshops for the business community, reaching 150 business owners and jump-starting our campaign.

"I invite you to make a donation tonight to make this dream a reality. If five individuals in this room each give $100, and twenty more each give $25, we will reach our goal. I want to draw your attention to the envelope and gift form under your seats. Please take a moment to fill this out—and give as generously as you can. While you're getting out your checkbook or credit card, I want to tell you a little bit more about our program."

At this point, take another minute to share some victories, highlights, or future plans, giving people time to pull out their cash or credit card or write a check. When your time is up, circulate a basket to collect donations.

You've probably noticed that in this sample ask, people heard exactly what the $1,000 contribution would make possible. This is a really important point. Will you be able to send five members of your team to a media training, print two thousand posters on recycled paper to advertise a local clean energy campaign, or rent office space for six months for your team? People are more likely to donate when they can imagine tangible results from their donation.

Another good strategy is to find someone ahead of time from within the group to whom you're presenting who is willing to make a pledge. If one person makes a public pledge, that often starts momentum that convinces other people to give, too.

When you are targeting individuals, you go about the ask in much the same way as for groups. Go into the meeting or phone call with a specific number in mind: usually double the amount that you think the person can give. First give the prospect your elevator pitch. Then make the ask and fall silent. "I'd like to invite you to donate $100 to our campaign today. Your

FUNDRAISING TIPS TO REMEMBER

If you don't ask, they won't give. This might sound silly, but it's true! People give when asked, plain and simple. Don't assume that donations will stream in just because you're doing a fantastic job on your campaign. You have to ask.

Get comfortable with no. You'll probably hear no more than you'll hear yes. As fundraising guru Kim Klein says in her online fundraising materials, "If you don't hear no several times a week, you are not asking enough people." Consider it a success if you're hearing no—that means you're doing your job as a fundraiser—and making lots of asks! Don't take it personally if someone says no, and never pressure people to give if they say no. Learn why they turned you down, and use that to improve your pitch or your targeting of potential donors.

Give people a starting point. Always suggest a donation amount, and make it higher than the amount you think they're able to comfortably give. That gives people a mental starting point for negotiation.

Make time for fundraising. Try to estimate the total number of hours needed to raise money, from writing letters to reaching out to prospective donors to meeting with people, then double or triple your estimate. Build this fundraising time into your campaign timeline and planning.

Say thank you in writing. Always thank your donors within two days of receiving your donation. Handwritten notes are great if you have a limited number of donors; if you have a ton, feel free to print out your letters, but write a line or two of personal thanks on the letter before putting it in the mail. This lets donors know that you received their money, reminds them about your cause, and is a key step in nurturing a long-term relationship.

Be in touch with your donors regularly—not just when you need money. Donors appreciate hearing about how your work is going throughout the year and don't want to only be asked for money during crunch time. Send emails or letters with campaign updates, including media clips, photographs from your campaign, or any additional materials your donors might find interesting.

Recognize your donors publicly. If you print any materials to hand out at events, ask your donors whether they are comfortable being listed as supporters.

contribution will help us print up a thousand postcards to deliver to the campus president, calling for a clean energy plan. What do you say?" Wait for the person's response.

One of your biggest assets as a fundraiser is to be a good listener. And good listening starts with silence. Silence is golden; it gives people time to think and time to respond. Give people time to say yes, or maybe to fully express any concerns. Really listening to people, rather than trying to pressure them into giving, is the key to making a connection that is genuine; it is your best chance for success as a fundraiser. If a prospect says no, ask whether he or she is willing to tell you why not, and use that response to help you improve your next ask, or to understand whether or not you can approach this person later when circumstances have changed.

If you're asking your peers for money, you'll probably set a smaller goal. Let's say you ask a friend for $10, and he tells you he can't afford it. Give him a sense of where he may already spend that money and how he can save the funds from that and reallocate it to your campaign. For instance, Rachel Barge helped convince fellow students at U.C. Berkeley to pledge $5 a semester to a sustainability fund by contextualizing it. "Five bucks is the cost of a burrito," she said. "Wouldn't you give up one burrito a semester to make U.C. Berkeley a sustainability leader?" Most students agreed with her logic and overwhelmingly voted during a campus election to give $10 each year to the new fund.

Finally, think outside the box. If someone can't offer financial resources, perhaps he can volunteer for your campaign, offer consulting services, make an in-kind donation (donations of goods or services like a used computer or legal assistance, rather than cash), or introduce you to friends who could donate. Come to any meeting prepared with a wish list of skills, services, and other items that your campaign needs in addition to money. Maybe your neighbor works for a company that has a matching gift program, whereby her company matches every donation their employees make to a nonprofit, or perhaps she knows someone who works for a foundation. If she can't give today but wants to support your cause, she may know other people you can ask or would be willing to host a house party and invite her friends to give.

Making the Ask: Follow Up

After you wrap up an in-person presentation or a phone call, send a follow-up letter (with a return donation envelope) or email (with a link to donate online) thanking the individual or group for their time, even if they didn't yet offer to donate. For people who donated during your presentation, make sure you send a personal thank-you note recognizing both their time and their financial contribution. Always follow up within two days of your conversation.

Still Afraid to Ask for Money?

If you're still feeling nervous about making your first request for money, ask yourself the following questions:

> ➤ Is my cause important enough to share it with the people I care about and members of my community?

> ➤ Would most people I know be sympathetic to my cause? Would they therefore be supportive of my group's mission?

> ➤ Does my group need money to function? If so, where do I think that money should come from?

> ➤ Is giving money to an environmental cause a bad thing or something people might actually enjoy and find great value in doing?

> ➤ Do I believe enough in my cause to take some personal social risks, including the possibility of getting rejected when I ask someone for money? Would the experience of getting rejected cause me to give up working for my organization or cause?

> ➤ What is really stopping me from asking my friends, family, and neighbors to support my cause?

Answering these questions honestly will help you understand why you may be hesitant to ask people for money and ideally will show you that fundraising can be a very positive experience. Your answers should also drive home the fact that fundraising is a vital activity for anyone who is working for a cause. The earlier you learn to face your fundraising fears, the more effective you'll be as a lifelong activist for social change. There are a number of training organizations that can help you overcome your fears and develop strong fundraising plans, including the Grassroots Institute for Fundraising Training, or GIFT (www.grassrootsfundraising.org). They have a great newsletter and tons of online resources, and they offer regular trainings.

OTHER SOURCES OF FINANCIAL SUPPORT

Beyond asking individual donors for support, the other main sources for social change funding include community and private foundations, government, corporations, and fundraising events. A number of student fundraising strategies are designed specifically for campus greening projects. These strategies all require time and effort to be successful, but it's often worth the work.

Foundations

A foundation is an organization that is created specifically to support an institution, or in some cases, many institutions or causes. Private foundations are created by individuals or families and typically distribute funds according to the values of the founding members. Community foundations, funded by families, individuals, businesses, and nonprofit groups in a particular region, typically give specifically to improve the quality of life in that city or county. Both private and community foundations often have a number of interests, from arts to education to the environment.

Unfortunately, private and community foundations aren't the most ideal sources of support for youth-led groups for a number of reasons. First, foundations usually have formal guidelines, and filling out the initial applications can be time-consuming, with no guarantee for funding. (As few as 10 percent of proposals actually receive funding.) Some foundations are closed to the public and invite only proposals based on personal relationships with groups and individuals. And nearly every foundation gives only to groups with 501(c)(3) status (see page 157). If you are lucky enough to be funded by a private foundation, you will probably be responsible for providing extensive reports and evaluations of your program.

If you think a foundation might be interested in your work, your first step after reviewing their funding guidelines online should be to approach the program officer dedicated to your area of interest. Reach out with a phone call and request an in-person or phone meeting to find out more about the foundation's giving and application process. The program officer can give you a better sense of your group's chances and give you the inside scoop on how to build a competitive application. You will need to spend nearly as much time researching the foundation and speaking with its staff to understand what kind of application might appeal to them as you do actually preparing application materials.

Foundation support requires a lot of relationship-building efforts and a lot of navigation, often through dense bureaucracy. Once you pass through the first gauntlet of getting a meeting with a program officer, the application materials can be quite dense and ask for very specific information that you may not yet have. For instance, what is the impact of your work? How many people does it stand to affect? What is the full cost of your project? Where will it be in ten years?

Foundations also can change their focus depending on the current economic, political, and social climate, or what their board of directors feels is a good investment. For these reasons, foundations are not ideal funding sources for youth-led groups. A more stable and consistent source of funding would be a group of individual donors or even a smaller family foundation that chooses some beloved signature projects. If you're nevertheless interested in further exploring this funding avenue, check out the Foundation Center (www.foundationcenter.org) for more resources and advice.

Government Funding

Obtaining government funds at the state and federal level often involves a burdensome application process, and the odds of success can be low. Like private and community foundations, government funding is typically not an ideal source for most youth groups.

If you would like to apply for federal or state government funding, find partners with lots of grant writing capacity and experience. Regional governmental funding sources can be much easier to navigate. Reach out to the mayor's office, and ask whether any such funding mechanisms exist for youth in your city or county. If so, typically you can get support from the office itself in preparing your application.

Corporate Donors

Businesses often earmark portions of their earnings to support community causes. If you find the right match, these corporate donors can be a great way to get substantive and relatively trouble-free donations. Although some businesses have involved application processes, others can be pitched with a simple email and phone call. Once I spent just two hours putting together materials and cold-calling an eco-oriented company to ask for support for the Brower Youth Awards. I was delighted to receive a donation of $5,000 with no formal grant reports or paperwork needed.

Although not every company donates to green causes—and those that do typically have limited resources—there are still many companies looking to support a good cause! Start by finding a good match. If the product or service that a company provides contradicts your environmental mission, it's obviously a poor match. Find a company you'd be proud to affiliate with. Not all companies will see your cause as worthy of support. Have your team do some brainstorming about companies that might be intrigued by your mission, then research their community giving programs to see what types of organizations and issues they support. Focus initially on companies in your city or region—companies are often most likely to give to local groups.

Identify the appropriate contact. Companies typically have departments that do community support. Find the community giving or community sponsorship department head and reach out to him with a letter and a follow-up phone call. Better yet, if you know anyone with ties to the company, ask for a personal introduction to their community giving department. Emails and letters alone often won't open a dialogue with a company, unless they've already heard about your work. Phone calls are better, and if you can't reach someone by phone but his office is located nearby, consider dropping off some materials and trying to meet with someone during your visit, if only to schedule a follow-up conversation.

Once you have snagged a meeting with the company, ask your contact what the company is looking for in a relationship with their partner organization—it's not just a one-way street. Is it looking to provide opportunities for its employees to get involved with the community? If so, offer volunteer workdays for the staff to partner with your group. Is it looking to market to a youth constituency? Figure out whether you can tactfully advertise its product or service at your events. You could also host a 5-percent sales day (on which 5 percent of all purchases go to your cause) and publicize this to your networks. Is the company looking for more brand recognition? List the company in your media releases and print materials as a sponsor. Or have the company brand itself through a matching grant. If you're able to raise a certain amount of funds, ask the company whether they'll match those funds with a donation of their own; every time you ask for a donation from others, you'll mention the company's matching grant, netting them some great feel-good publicity.

If the company decides to give, you'll want to maintain the relationship. It's much easier to go back to a company year after year for funding than to find new donors each year. Keep them updated on your work on a year-round basis, not just when you need money, and ask them to tell you honestly how they felt about their contribution to and investment in your group after big events or campaign pushes.

Fundraising Events

Another fundraising strategy is to host an event. Although it's usually more time-consuming to plan an event than it is to ask an individual or a company for funds, events not only raise money but also create the opportunity for you to grow people who will actively support your organization as volunteers and ongoing advocates. Here's just a handful of the best ideas I've come across for fundraising events:

➤ Raise money for your organization by running a Better World Books (www.betterworldbooks.com) book drive; they will pay your group for each qualifying book and will redistribute your books to nonprofit literacy programs.

➤ Find a local restaurant that will donate a portion of a particular day's profits to your group, and help them promote the event. Ask your friends, family, and everyone you know to frequent the restaurant that day—they get a great meal, and you get a sweet check.

➤ Are you or another member of your team an expert cook, a published poet, or a phenomenal painter? Offer to teach your skills—activist or otherwise—to community members and donate the proceeds to your organization. You can make hundreds or thousands of dollars in a few hours (plus the time to promote and plan the workshop).

➤ Get items donated, or better yet, gather the masterpieces produced from your peers, and sell your own creations, especially if they're eco-friendly. This is particularly well timed for the holiday gift-giving season.

➤ Your junk is another person's treasure! Ask group members to contribute all the stuff gathering dust in their closets, and then sell it on eBay or host a big garage sale with all proceeds benefitting your cause.

➤ Host a house party or dinner. Charge a cover for everyone attending, or let people know that it's a free event, but you'll make a financial ask at the end of the night. Phebe Meyers used this strategy to set up an annual fundraiser that nets her organization more than $10,000 in just one night.

SUCCESS STORY
FOREVER FOREST Growing up in Woodstock, Vermont, eighteen-year-old **Phebe Meyers** noticed fewer songbirds at her feeders each year. After doing a little research, she discovered the cause: the deforestation of migratory bird corridors (once stunning rainforests) in Costa Rica was affecting the number of songbirds everywhere. She shared her concern about the crisis with Change the World Kids, a teen-run nonprofit organization she cofounded in 1998 with her twin sister, Nika.

When Phebe learned that it would take more than a million dollars to purchase and reforest the migratory corridor in Costa Rica, she got started fundraising. One of her first techniques was hosting a series of events over one weekend, consisting of a kids' game night, a concert, a silent auction, an art show, and a dinner.

The dinner was located at a local restaurant that was very engaged in supporting environmental initiatives. Phebe met with the owners and chef, who offered to donate the full proceeds from the cost of the dinner, $100 per person, to the campaign. Her team asked local farms and food purveyors to donate produce. They sent out invitations to the restaurant's mailing list, their own donor list, and friends and families of the group members, ultimately bringing together seventy-five diners.

Her group set up a silent auction at the dinner, offering donated items, services, or trips from both Costa Rican and local stores and individuals. Interested individuals could write their names on a sheet of paper, bidding silently; at the end of the evening, the highest bidder for each item won. The guests milled around the room in the beginning of the event, enjoying food and the silent auction. After her team's first weekend raised $12,000, they made it an annual event, eventually bringing in $32,000 in one weekend.

Through years of additional fundraising efforts, Phebe's group raised over $200,000 to help purchase, conserve, and reforest an area critical to indigenous birds and neotropical migrants. They named the corridor Bosque para Siempre, or Forever Forest.

"The need **TO ACCEPT DONATIONS** for Bosque para Siempre led me to **ESTABLISH A 501[C][3] NONPROFIT ORGANIZATION**. I learned to keep basic fundraising records, use an accounting program, and do our banking and financial reports. Now I act as a financial advisor." **—PHEBE MEYERS**

Not only did Phebe host an annual dinner as a fundraiser, but her team also used an enormous number of creative strategies, including the following:

➤ Sales of Fair Trade coffee from a Costa Rican cooperative

➤ Week-long service trips to Costa Rica rainforests, with the trip fees supporting the project

➤ A carbon footprint program that lets people offset their travel carbon emissions with donations to the Bosque para Siempre reforestation program

➤ A concert of local youth musicians called "Bonk for the Bellbirds"

➤ A night of rainforest games for young kids, including a life-size "Waterfalls and Vines" game based on Chutes and Ladders, as well as a rainforest cafe featuring Costa Rican foods

➤ A partnership with the Costa Rican Conservation Foundation to apply for, and receive, two matching grants from the U.S. Fish and Wildlife Service

If you want to raise the big bucks, similar to Change the World Kids, you should plan to experiment with multiple strategies until you find the events that resonate best with the people in your community—then make these an annual or ongoing affair. One-time events that change year after year aren't as effective as finding one successful event (or more!) that you can brand and repeat.

STARTING YOUR OWN NONPROFIT

Like Phebe, if you plan to fundraise, either seek a fiscal sponsor or become your own 501(c)(3), otherwise known as a nonprofit. A primary reason for seeking 501(c)(3) status or fiscal sponsorship is that you want your donors to be able to take a tax deduction for the gifts they give you. For some donors, this is a significant incentive to give. And some people will feel more confident giving your group money knowing that you are part of a legal organization, with financial records that are regularly examined by the government.

If you're ready to form a 501(c)(3), you should consult a lawyer for advice and read other resources on the subject, like the book *How to Form a Nonprofit Corporation* by attorney Anthony Mancuso (Nolo, 2009).

You'll need to select an available business name, file formal paperwork, apply for federal and state tax exemptions, create corporate bylaws (operating rules for your nonprofit), set up a board of directors, and obtain any necessary licenses and permits. This is the perfect time to seek pro bono (free) advice from a lawyer in town that specializes in nonprofit corporations.

Starting your own nonprofit is an enormous undertaking; research it extensively to make sure this is the right step for your group. Applying

READY TO LAUNCH? HERE'S HELP

Some programs focus on helping other new nonprofits grow and expand their impact, providing funding and organizational development coaching. Echoing Green (www.echoinggreen.org) offers a fellowship program for social entrepreneurs who are starting a new organization. Fellows receive financial support, technical assistance, and access to a network of social change-makers over multiple years. Dell's Social Innovation Competition (www.dellsocialinnovation competition.com) helps college students worldwide perfect a business or project plan, pitch their idea to investors, and build a network of supporters.

for (and then maintaining) your own nonprofit status requires ongoing attention and time; thus, it's best for large, long-term projects.

FISCAL SPONSORSHIP

A fiscal sponsor is a nonprofit that assumes the legal and financial responsibility for multiple groups' operations. Earth Island Institute is a fiscal sponsor that has helped birth and support more than a hundred projects since its inception as a nonprofit. Each fiscal sponsor offers particular benefits; the benefits of joining Earth Island Institute's project network are 501(c)(3) status, gaining credibility in the public's eye by becoming part of an organization that's been around for decades, presence on a website, and accounting and payroll services. Perhaps the most valuable benefit is access to experienced staff members who have worked with a number of new organizations over decades and can help advise you in all aspects of growing your group.

Fiscal sponsors charge a fee for their services, which usually ranges from 7 to 15 percent of your incoming funds—and a fiscal sponsor will not typically fundraise for you. Determine what services and support you need from a sponsor, then see which sponsors offer that package of services for a reasonable fee. Remember that everything costs money: if you're not paying a fiscal sponsor, then you may have to pay an outside accountant and lawyer to ensure that your organization is operating responsibly and within the law.

Working with a fiscal sponsor is typically best for small or part-time activist groups that don't have the funds, capacity, or desire to hire their own accountant and build a board of directors (a group of outside advisors that meets regularly to help manage the organization and chart its direction). Fiscal sponsorship can be a temporary step toward gaining 501(c)(3) status, or you can keep your fiscal sponsor for the life of your organization.

You can search by region and under the youth category at the Fiscal Sponsor Directory (www.fiscalsponsordirectory.org), a resource designed to connect community projects with fiscal sponsors. Phebe Meyers launched her own nonprofit as a minor; Adarsha Shivakumar found his time and energy better used in searching for a partner to be his fiscal sponsor.

SUCCESS STORY
PROJECT JATROPHA Fourteen-year-old **Adarsha Shivakumar**
cofounded Project Jatropha with his sister Apoorva to promote the plant *Jatropha curcas* as an ecologically friendly and economically sustainable source of plant-based biofuel in rural India. Project Jatropha collaborated with Parivarthana, a nonprofit that helps farmers, and Labland Biotechs, a plant biotechnology company, to convince farmers that raising *Jatropha* was an economically sustainable project.

After demonstrating the conversion of *Jatropha* seeds into biofuel, Adarsha's team distributed the biofuel so that farmers could test it on their irrigation pumps. The results were clear: the biofuel burned cleaner and worked smoother than the diesel that had previously been used. Armed with this knowledge, farmers set about planting the one thousand *Jatropha* seedlings that Project Jatropha had purchased for them, using the money Adarsha earned by winning a California spelling bee.

Their project progressed rapidly, and teammate Callie Roberts suggested that Project Jatropha apply for nonprofit status. Adarsha and Apoorva made several trips to banks, bought books about starting a nonprofit organization, and contacted attorneys. Time and again, they discovered that their age was an obstacle to launching a nonprofit. So instead, Adarsha found a partner with its own nonprofit status, Sirona Cares Foundation, to become their fiscal sponsor.

"My advice for folks under eighteen: do not try to start an independent nonprofit. **RESEARCH ORGANIZATIONS DOING SIMILAR WORK AND APPROACH THEM**, as there is a good chance that they will be able to help you."

—ADARSHA SHIVAKUMAR

FUNDING FOR COLLEGE AND UNIVERSITY STUDENTS

All of the fundraising strategies just detailed can be used for any project. However, if you're raising big money for college and university greening projects, there are a number of additional fundraising mechanisms available.

Rachel Barge saw that the single biggest factor limiting sustainability projects on campus was a lack of seed funding. Instead of waiting for the campus to provide the funds, she turned to the student body to implement a student sustainability fee, a tactic that has been used successfully time and time again on college and university campuses.

SUCCESS STORY

TGIF   As an undergrad at U.C. Berkeley, eighteen-year-old **Rachel Barge** sat on the Chancellor's Advisory Committee on Sustainability. The committee published an $80,000 Campus Sustainability Assessment when she was a freshman. The report was basically the how-to guide to make her campus more sustainable in every area: energy, water, transportation, and buildings. Rachel watched the document gather dust on a shelf for two years because the university lacked funds to implement most of the project suggestions. Rachel and some friends decided that students needed to act first, to show the administration that the student body was serious about seeing the assessment implemented. She figured that if students could dig extra money out of their own pockets, the campus could at least match the funds.

Her student fee campaign was called The Green Initiative Fund, or TGIF. TGIF was a mandatory fee passed by the student body in 2007, charging $5 per student per semester for a ten-year period. This raised $200,000 per year or $2,000,000 over ten years for sustainability projects on campus, including clean energy, sustainable transportation, improved energy efficiency, water conservation, green internships, and improved recycling and composting programs.

The fund was overseen by a committee consisting of staff and students; in the first year, their "request for proposals" from the campus generated a staggering $1.4 million in requests. The biggest project funded in the first year was a Campus Dashboard program to monitor all electricity use on-site in campus buildings, so staff and energy managers could determine where energy efficiency programs and retrofits were most needed.

"A SMALL CONTRIBUTION CAN MAKE A BIG DIFFERENCE in combating tangible problems on campus." **—RACHEL BARGE**

© Drew Altizer

Student-initiated campus funds like TGIF can tackle the next generation of clean energy deployment, green infrastructure investment, and educational transformation on your campus. Campus funds finally make possible expensive large-scale projects such as upgrades and technology investments. And because they are student-initiated, the funds are often student-controlled, meaning students are empowered to truly effect change on their campus.

Student fees have become one of the most successful strategies to raise funds for sustainability and empower students as change-makers on their campus. Students at more than fifty U.S. colleges and universities have approved "green fee" increases to fund major, institution-wide, and student-directed sustainability and energy initiatives. Depending on the size of the student body and the amount of the fee, funds can range from tens of thousands to millions of dollars. Most fees generally fall between $5 and $20 per student per semester and create funds of $10,000 to $200,000 annually.

The most common process for increasing fees is by passing a referendum on a student government or student body voting ballot, whereby a majority of the student population agrees to pay a fee increase. If successful, this measure is usually reviewed by a committee of administrators or financial managers and approved by the final decision-making authority, such as the board of regents or trustees. At other schools, proposing a student fee increase may be as simple as taking it directly to the committee rather than passing a referendum.

After her success, Rachel started getting lots of questions and requests for advice from students who were in critical need of funds for campus greening projects. So she wrote "Raise the Funds," an action guide to help college and university students across the country design and create large campus funds. It offers unique models for creating funds, ranging from tens of thousands to several million dollars each, that can fund any improvements your campus needs. Following is an overview of a handful of Rachel's strategies along with some successful student case studies. You can find many more ideas in Rachel's tool kit (see Resources).

Revolving Loan Funds (RLFs)

This is a pool of money set aside to finance campus projects that will actually save money or generate revenue for the campus. Unlike grant funds, money "revolves" through this fund, and a portion of the returns from projects is reinvested into the fund until the project has been entirely paid off. Because of the financial incentives, it's much easier to convince the administration to front the initial financial investment. Timothy DenHerder-Thomas of Macalester College in Minnesota knew that one of the best ways to convince the administration to fund going green was to speak to the eventual cost savings.

PROFITING FROM CLIMATE SOLUTIONS

Timothy DenHerder-Thomas wanted to find a way to invest in campus greening projects that would save the campus money and reduce carbon emissions. He believed the project-by-project basis in which student campaigns often operate—making one change and then needing to start back at square one for the next—was slow and ineffective.

So Timothy cocreated the Macalester College Clean Energy Revolving Fund (CERF), a fund to finance profitable sustainability projects and recapture the savings or revenue created to grow the fund. Timothy sought financial support from student government and an academic department, initially raising $27,000 for projects, and set up a board of students, faculty, administration, and alumni to select the campus greening projects. The fund allowed Macalester College to pilot water conservation, building insulation, and appliance efficiency projects, while rolling out a full-campus retrofit of fluorescent lighting, saving more than $40,000 annually and hundreds of tons of carbon emissions.

Eventually, with cost savings reinvested (and additional financial commitments made by the campus), the fund grew to more than $100,000. The project helped change the frame of how administrators approached sustainability from one of cost to one of smart financial investment, and became the inspiration for similar funds on college campuses across the United States.

© Han Shan

"As long as sustainability is perceived as sacrifice, it will be fatally limited in scope. My work reframes and then demonstrates **CLIMATE SOLUTIONS** as **BOLD OPPORTUNITIES** for economic profit." **—TIMOTHY DENHERDER-THOMAS**

Timothy had to find seed money for the fund, so he looked to both student government (which usually has established guidelines for distributing funds to student projects and groups) and an academic department. To seek funding from academic departments, you might start by requesting a meeting with the department chair or dean. In addition to those resources, you can seek funds from the following sources on college and university campuses: endowed chairs, college deans, the chancellor or president of the university, and career placement centers. Ask the campus's development officer to host a fundraising 101 workshop for your group, helping you to develop a strategy that is likely to work on your campus (and build a fundraising ally in the process).

Alumni Groups

If you find that your campus administration or students aren't good sources for funds, look to your campus's alumni. Alumni can be valuable allies in pushing for green initiatives on college and university campuses (and sometimes at K–12 schools), as well as a potential source of funding for the projects themselves. Donating to green projects might appeal to alumni who would not otherwise consider donating to the campus.

Alumni networks can also be tremendously useful for guidance, mentoring, technical and consulting expertise, and connections to industry, and as an additional source of pressure for sustainability initiatives. Depending on the alumni pool, potential funding can range from thousands of dollars to millions of dollars. For students who are graduating—and about to become alumni—you can set up a "senior gift"; this money raised from outgoing students will fund a green project that the graduates will leave behind as their legacy to the school.

INVESTING IN THE FUTURE

By asking people to support your work, you're giving them an opportunity to put their money where their hearts are, not to mention investing in something crucial to the greening of our society—you and your team! This chapter has introduced you to a number of strategies for funding your campaigns; these are just the tip of the iceberg. Use your creativity to think of more ideas. Can you sell a service or product your team makes? That's a great way to ease yourself away from being dependent on donors and to make your work self-sustaining. You could sell energy-efficient lightbulbs, food produced in your community garden, tool kits and books compiled by your team, and so much more.

No matter what fundraising tactics you choose, think carefully about how much time and effort they will require, plus any related expenses. Events, especially, can often take tons of hours to plan and execute, and sometimes the financial returns are disappointing. If you make $1,000 from a community dinner party, that's great, right? But if you had to spend $300 on food and supplies and it took three months to plan and advertise, you probably could have made the same funds easier and faster by reaching out to local businesses or individuals in your community. Time is money, as they say. So use yours wisely!

NEXT STOP: GREEN YOUR CAMPUS

Speaking of raising money for campus projects, if you're a student, the next chapter is for you. It shares lots of ideas for greening four sectors of your campus: facilities, curricula, food, and transportation. Making your school more sustainable is a great way to make a difference at the local level.

If you aren't currently attending school, don't worry. Many of the greening ideas in the next chapter can be applied to government agencies, private businesses, homeowners, nonprofits in the community, and more.

RESOURCES

Achieving Excellence in Fundraising by Hank Rosso, 3rd edition. San Francisco, CA: Jossey Bass, 2010.

Campus InPower, www.campusinpower.org Designed by BYA recipient Rachel Barge, this website details successful fundraising strategies (and offers a downloadable tool kit) for students at colleges and universities that want to implement new green projects. Rachel has helped more than fifty campuses develop funding strategies to support their new initiatives.

Captain Planet, www.captainplanetfoundation.org Captain Planet funds hands-on projects that address environmental problems in your neighborhood and community. Grant awards vary, but are usually between $250 and $2,500.

Clinton Global Initiative University (CGIU), www.cgiu.org/funding CGIU gives grants of up to $10,000 annually to more than a dozen projects focusing on energy and climate change or a slew of other global issues.

Do Something, www.dosomething.org Do Something offers $500 grants to the under-twenty-five crowd launching new initiatives, as well as opportunities for funding of up to $100,000!

Earth Island Institute, www.earthisland.org Earth Island Institute offers fiscal sponsorship and organizational development assistance to environmental projects, and has helped incubate more than a hundred projects since 1982, including youth-led projects.

Foundation Center, www.foundationcenter.org The Foundation Center hosts a fantastic database on U.S. grantmakers (available online for a fee or through state partners like libraries) and offers free and affordable educational and training programs.

Grassroots Institute for Fundraising Training (GIFT), www.grass rootsfundraising.org GIFT builds the capacity of progressive organizations to raise money, offering great online and print resources and many trainings.

Soul of Money, www.soulofmoney.org The Soul of Money Institute offers workshops and coaching for organizations and individuals to create freedom and power in their relationship with money. Check out founder Lynne Twist's powerful book, *The Soul of Money* (Norton, 2006).

Successful Fundraising: A Complete Handbook for Volunteers and Professionals by Joan Flanagan. Columbus, OH: McGraw-Hill, 2002.

Youth Service America (YSA), www.ysa.org/grants YSA distributes more than 400 micro grants each year for service and service-learning initiatives. Most of the grants support projects that culminate on Global Youth Service Day in April.

Youth Venture, www.youthventure.org Youth Venture offers seed grants of up to $1,000 for teams of young people (with a point person between age twelve and twenty) who are launching new "ventures."

10
GREEN YOUR CAMPUS
IDEAS TO CREATE A MORE SUSTAINABLE SCHOOL

ampuses are the epicenters of environmental change, and for good reason. With fifty-five million K-12 students and four million faculty members in the United States, over 20 percent of the country's population goes to school five days a week. More than $550 billion is spent on the education of these K-12 students. Add another eighteen million college and university students, and you're looking at about seventy-three million students (not to mention faculty and teachers) and hundreds of billions of dollars spent on and within educational institutions. Those are some huge numbers!

Campuses spend enormous sums of money on all sorts of products—cars and buses, electricity, building supplies, paper, and food, to name just a handful. Wouldn't it be great if we could use this money to create green jobs instead of dumping our dollars into dirty industries? Each time a campus makes a new environmental commitment, like buying 100 percent renewable energy instead of coal energy, we support the creation of a green economy. This chapter shares ideas for reducing your K-12 or college campus's ecological footprint in four areas where students can make the biggest difference: facilities, sustainability education, food, and transportation. If every campus greened one of these areas, imagine the impact!

So why are schools some of the best places to launch a green movement? The initiatives that start on campuses frequently serve as models for cities, states, and nations at large. If you save your campus $40,000 annually in an energy retrofit, you can export that model and help local businesses and government agencies do the same. Also, students carry lessons learned through campus greening projects into the workforce after graduation—as they take on roles as future politicians, engineers, advocates, and scientists (ideally with sustainability in mind!).

Don't believe that your work on campus could become a model for cities, states, and even the nation? Consider Billy Parish, cofounder of the Energy Action Coalition, a grassroots, youth-run nonprofit dedicated to addressing climate change. Here's how he and his group were able to have a huge impact on the clean energy movement in North America by starting locally: on campus.

SUCCESS STORY
THE CAMPUS CLIMATE CHALLENGE When Billy Parish
went to India the summer after his sophomore year at Yale, he thought that doing research on community reforestry practices would be the perfect introduction to the international economic development work he hoped to do after graduation. But during his four months there he got a different type of educational experience—one that changed his life.

One day Billy hiked to the Gaumukh glacier, a pilgrimage site for many Hindus. The glacier, set in the foothills of the Himalaya Mountains, is the source of the sacred Ganges River—a river that supports about four hundred million people. When Billy arrived at the glacier, he discovered a team of Indian scientists who informed him that the glacier was melting due to global warming. The lifeblood of a continent was at risk of running dry.

Billy suddenly got it—the work he needed to be doing wasn't in India, halfway around the world from his home. To fight against global warming and prevent this glacier from melting, he had to make change in his own country.

His first task on returning home was to help bring together the different threads of the campus sustainability movement in the Northeast. He co-organized a leadership summit, with more than sixty students from thirty schools meeting to figure out how to work more closely together. Out of this meeting emerged the Energy Action Coalition—an umbrella group for student groups and activists tackling climate change.

Like most social movements, Energy Action got off to a modest start. In late 2003, sixteen national college environmental groups came together for the first Campus Clean Energy Day to raise awareness about the threat of climate change. Then more organizations got involved, and in the spring of 2004 about thirty groups organized a Fossil Fools Day on campuses nationwide.

In 2006, Energy Action crafted the Campus Climate Challenge to spur a new wave of investment in renewable energy on college campuses from coast to coast. The movement kept growing, with days of action and campus organizing, and the Climate Challenge is now being run on more than seven hundred colleges and universities across the country. More than 550 of those campuses have made institutional commitments to become carbon neutral.

"How did we **BUILD THE LARGEST CAMPUS ENVIRONMENTAL COALITION**, which today includes more than fifty organizations in the U.S. and Canada? The old-fashioned way: through the **HARD WORK** of community organizing." **—BILLY PARISH**

Although Billy's group originally set out only to make an impact on university and college campuses, they soon found out that they were growing into a national political force. They brought together twelve thousand students in Washington, D.C., for the Power Shift 2009 summit, where students spoke at congressional hearings and six thousand students descended upon Capitol Hill for the largest lobby day focused on clean energy by youth in American history. So although your efforts might start small, who knows how they'll grow, and what types of models you'll create for systematic change in your city, state, nation, or world?

Focusing on clean energy isn't the only way to make a difference on campus. This chapter details a number of opportunities. Once you've found an idea that looks promising, go to Earth Day Network's Green Your School site (www.earthday.org/greenyourschool) to find tried-and-true action plans for success. Or adapt the model from chapter 2 to design your own plan for any of the issues mentioned in this chapter.

Campus administrators are usually happy to have students initiate new projects. After all, the more work you do in driving new projects forward, the easier their jobs are, right? But there are some ideal ways for students to approach working with campus administrators.

WORKING WITH CAMPUS ADMINISTRATORS

Being prepared is a necessity when working with officials, representatives, or professionals of any kind. Be persuasive and thorough. Show the people in charge that you've thought through your project. Include the benefit to students and staff, a budget, and a suggested list of supplies, staff time, and specific support needed from the school.

> ➤ Save some dough: Financial returns will make your project much more appealing. If you can save money with your project, estimate the total cost to launch and long-term savings for the school. If the project will cost money, offer suggestions on sources of financing, such as fundraisers, grants, reallocation of unused funds from other programs, or community support. Focus on how to make this source of revenue renewable, so the school doesn't have to start from scratch year after year for ongoing costs.

> ➤ Get the right parties involved from the start: If your project involves the dining services staff, invite them to meet early on during your action planning; the same goes for the grounds maintenance and janitorial staffs, budgeting managers, campus sustainability coordinators, the principal, or any other party with a stake in the issue. Present your initial ideas during a short meeting with key

players and get a read on the level of support or opposition you'll encounter.

➤ Ask questions: Don't do all the talking. Make sure you understand any questions or concerns the administrators may have about your project. Knowing more about their perspective helps you present a more compelling case.

➤ Leverage the student body: Use class talks, assemblies, and campus meetings to educate the student body and build support for your cause. If at first you don't succeed, grow a bigger pool of supporters. Remind the faculty who they are there to serve: you!

➤ Keep a paper trail: Retain copies of all emails, faxes, and letters you send, with dates. This is helpful to track progress (or lack of it), particularly if the campus administration is failing to live up to their promises.

➤ Appreciation goes a long way: Thank the faculty for meeting with you. Thank them for reviewing your proposal. Thank them for giving you funds to launch the project. In short, you can never offer too many thank-yous.

➤ Report back: It's necessary to measure your accomplishments against the goals you set out for yourself, and to gauge how much energy, water, money, or other precious resources you're saving for the school—and the planet!

➤ Share your victory: Imagine if every campus in your state implemented the same green changes you did—what a huge, collective victory! Once you've tackled green projects on your own campus, mentor other campuses, organizations, or businesses to do the same, whether locally or nationally.

What if you do everything right, by your account, but your campus administration won't budge? Administrators may create obstacles for your group, so be prepared to wage your battle with a plethora of tactics, strategies, and patience to win your campaign.

Dealing with Obstacles

If you encounter any significant impediments, stay friendly, respectful, and calm. Getting on an administrator's bad side to prove a point won't help you in the long run. Don't challenge an administrator alone; use diplomacy. Find allies—other teachers, parents, and fellow students—to assist in advocating for your group. Talk to other activists and leaders on campus about how they have navigated difficult campus relationships.

If an administrator challenges your right to host a campus event or launch a new project, make a strong case for how your event or project will promote education and thoughtful dialogue about an important environmental issue. Anticipate their concerns, and come prepared with appropriate responses. When possible, address their concerns by citing the values or mission of your school. Your administrator may have additional concerns; discuss possible ways to alleviate these concerns, and be prepared to do more research. If other schools have hosted similar events or programs, be prepared to give successful examples and make the case that your campus is falling behind. College campuses and private high schools, particularly, are sensitive to enhancing their reputations. Use that to your advantage.

If you get stuck at the campus administration level, can you take your appeal to another body? Perhaps the school board, city council, or PTA will hear out your proposal. Ask campus media, sympathetic adult allies, or parents and friends to weigh in. High schools are governed by school boards, which make decisions on anything from school budgets to campus curricula. You can contact school board members individually or get onto the agenda for an upcoming meeting. Make sure you're not alone; invite your supporters to attend the meeting as well, even if they cannot speak—you demonstrate strength in numbers.

Finally, if all official channels lead to dead ends, escalate your campaign. Demonstrate irrefutable campus support for your campaign, using tactics such as a statement of support signed by a portion of the campus body and parents.

Now that you've got some ideas on how to build positive working relationships and resolve challenges that arise as you begin campus organizing, it's time to get started with specific greening initiatives. Let's start with facilities.

GREENING YOUR FACILITIES

Did you know that buildings consume 72 percent of our electricity while emitting approximately 39 percent of carbon emissions? Beyond that, school building construction represents the largest construction sector in America, totaling $80 billion between 2006 and 2008—about 27 percent of America's construction market.

Despite the fact that upon graduation the average student has spent more than twenty-four thousand hours in largely unhealthy buildings, the greening of our buildings is not a priority in campus budgets. This is especially unfortunate considering that campus-wide conservation efforts—such as installing renewable energy systems or energy-efficient products, maximizing natural light indoors, and using green roofs—can significantly improve the health and learning environments for students and also save campuses thousands of dollars. Those who regularly spend time in clean, green buildings with healthy food and access to the outdoors have lower rates of asthma and respiratory problems, diabetes, and obesity, and even perform better academically.

There are five main areas for reducing your campus's environmental footprint in terms of facilities: renewable energy and energy efficiency, water conservation, sustainable buildings, reducing and recycling waste, and purchasing green products for use in the classrooms. Usually energy and water efficiency are the easiest places to start, because it's a no-brainer for the campus—saving resources saves money.

Start with energy, one of the mostly costly items in a campus budget. The nation's K–12 school districts spend more than $6 billion a year on energy, more than what is spent on computers and textbooks combined. A lot of that energy production is unnecessary—by making efficiency improvements in our buildings, schools could save more than 25 percent of the energy currently used on-site. And the wasted money could go to more important things, like education itself. It's estimated that with a 25-percent reduction in energy costs, the savings could pay for thirty thousand new teacher salaries, forty million textbooks, or hundreds of thousands of computers!

Audit Your School's Energy Usage

It is up to you to show your administrators how much money and energy they are wasting. Energy audits investigate the energy use and the efficiency of your building, from the kinds of lightbulbs used to the hours of unnecessary electronics use. Having hard data in hand will make it very difficult for your campus's administration to ignore your suggestions for green improvements.

Clean Air-Cool Planet's Campus Carbon Calculator (www.cleanaircoolplanet.org) offers detailed instructions and guidance for running an audit on your campus and is the tool used by most of the six-hundred-plus signatories to the American College and University Presidents' Climate Commitment (www.presidentsclimatecommitment.org), a voluntary agreement to move toward campus climate neutrality. Earth Day Network similarly offers a classroom lighting audit and calculator tool for K–12 schools to calculate their school's lighting footprint (www.earthday.org/lighting). After you know where your campus is wasting the most energy, develop an action plan for a lighting retrofit or implement any number of resource-saving measures: getting energy from renewable energy sources, shutting down and unplugging electronics when not in use, replacing lighting systems with energy-efficient bulbs, installing green roofs (roofs partially or completely covered with vegetation that reduce the need for campus heating or cooling, depending on the design), or outreach to encourage students to make behavioral changes like using natural light when available.

Heating, Ventilation, and Air Conditioning (HVAC) Systems

Campus heating during the winters is a big deal, particularly in cold climates; students simply can't learn without heat. If your campus relies on a petroleum-based HVAC system, you can promote alternatives to global warming–causing fuels. Jessie-Ruth Corkins found a way to heat her school without using fossil fuels and to save money in the process.

SUCCESS STORY

BURNING FOR CHANGE
It started with $100—an innocent challenge from **Jessie-Ruth Corkins's** ninth grade earth science teacher, Mr. Tailer. He offered cash from his own pocket to students who could come up with a greener, more environmentally friendly way to heat Mount Abraham Union High School in Bristol, Vermont.

Jessie-Ruth and her friend Christi Kroll stepped up to the plate. Little did they know that their simple science project would end up becoming a major environmental, social, and political issue—and not just for their high school, but for the whole state of Vermont!

Jessie-Ruth started by making phone calls to research renewable heating options and discovered that burning wood chips instead of oil would be the best fit for her school. The wood could be harvested in her town and trucked to the school from only half a mile away. The process of using a locally harvested fuel burned in stoves that were partially manufactured in Vermont would reduce the school's carbon footprint.

Once she discovered this was the best option, she had to look at the economics and what it would cost to retire the two oil burners that were already in the school. She called the local oil company to find out how much the school had spent for five years of heating and compared it to the price of wood chips, which turned out to be cheaper. Considering that oil prices were projected to keep increasing, wood chips offered a lower, more stable price for fuel. But she still needed to figure out a way to pay for the initial cost of buying and installing a new wood chip furnace, which would cost nearly $2 million.

Jessie-Ruth and Christi got a break when they discovered a state grant offering 90 percent aid to fund renewable energy projects in Vermont public schools. That meant only 10 percent would come out of local taxpayers' pockets. This was huge! Nineteen other schools in Vermont had already switched to wood chips using these grants, so they had a strong track record to use in their efforts.

Jessie-Ruth lobbied local constituents leading up to Town Meeting Day, when local residents elected their town officials and passed local budgets. She spent the day passing out flyers and talking to people on the street, trying to get them to understand and approve the project. In the end, the voters approved the project by a very slim margin.

"Since the wood chip furnace was installed, it has **KEPT MORE THAN 500 TONS OF NEW CARBON EMISSIONS FROM** being added to **THE ATMOSPHERE**. By the time I was a senior, savings had tripled—to $90,000 per year. We had succeeded!" **—JESSIE-RUTH CORKINS**

In addition to wasting energy in classrooms and with HVAC systems, campuses are huge water hogs. The good news is there are many easy ways to reduce your campus's water consumption.

Reducing Water Use

While 1.3 billion people on the planet don't have access to safe drinking water, an enormous amount of America's potable water supply is used for things like watering lawns or flushing toilets. For example, six thousand gallons of water will be used daily at the average size middle school, simply to flush toilets! Just as it requires tons of water to collect and transport energy, it also takes a lot of energy to collect, clean, and transport water. Plus, although freshwater supply is finite, global water demand doubles every twenty years, at more than twice the rate of human population growth. Pollution and overextraction in many regions of the world has reduced the ability of water supplies to meet the growing demand. In the coming decades, water shortages will become a major worldwide problem affecting practically every nation on earth. As a result, water efficiency is an easy and money-saving green measure to conserve such a precious resource!

Audits can be helpful tools in this case as well, to assess the water usage (and wastage) on your campus. Once you identify the biggest water hogs, here are some ways to be water-conscious:

➤ Install rain shut-off devices on sprinkler systems.

➤ Adjust the water used seasonally.

➤ Use drip irrigation systems instead of sprinklers.

➤ Irrigate at night rather than during the heat of the day.

➤ Apply mulch to help retain soil moisture, so the area will require less watering.

➤ Install rainwater catchment systems as an alternative water supply, with rainwater collected and stored for future use on school grounds.

➤ Convince your campus to replace grass and exotic plant species with regionally appropriate plants whenever possible.

➤ Landscape with the native plants that thrive in your local area, which eliminates the need for chemical supplements and requires minimal maintenance from the grounds staff. In addition, they provide habitat for local wildlife. If you live in a dry, arid area, be sure to use drought-tolerant plants.

➤ Convert old toilets to low-flush toilets or no-flush urinals.

Meet with the campus grounds and facilities staff to develop an action plan for reducing water use outdoors and indoors in the existing facilities. Then look at how you can green new buildings or ensure that new renovations incorporate green principles.

Greening Your Buildings

Green building refers to the construction of buildings that maximize environmentally responsible and resource-efficient measures throughout a building's life cycle: from selecting the location to its design, construction, operation, maintenance, and renovation. When your campus plans to construct new buildings or renovate existing ones, use your leverage as a student to persuade them to use eco-friendly building materials and energy- and water-efficient design. Particularly if you pay tuition on campus (or are paying a special fee for new campus buildings), investigate where this money is going and demand that it be spent in more sustainable ways, as Eugene Pearson did at the University of Colorado.

SUCCESS STORY
FROM BUDGET CRISIS TO THE GREENEST
BUILDING STANDARDS When a budget crisis forced the state

to cut education funding, University of Colorado at Boulder officials turned
to its student council to enact a fee hike to finance the construction of four
new campus buildings. Led by then-junior **Eugene Pearson**, the student
council did just this. As a condition of its support, the student council
insisted that new campus construction meet green building standards and
that 100 percent of the electricity for the new buildings come from renewable resources. After Eugene's analysis showed that the new building's rate
of return would be ten times the university's investment, university officials
signed on, making CU-Boulder's building standards some of the greenest
in the country.

© Eugene Pearson

"We were able to demonstrate that **CAREFUL PLANNING,
THOUGHTFUL DESIGN,** and **INVESTMENT IN
SUSTAINABLE PRACTICES** are good for the pocketbook
and the environment." **–EUGENE PEARSON**

Eugene relied on standards developed by the U.S. Green Building
Council, a nonprofit working to make green buildings available to everyone
within a generation. They coordinate the Leadership in Energy and Environmental Design (LEED) program, an internationally recognized green
building certification system, which can be applied to existing buildings via
retrofits and improvements, or to new buildings. Learn more about how to
green your campus facilities at www.greenschoolbuildings.org.

The environmental impact of campus classrooms and facilities extends
far beyond their walls, including the incoming supplies and the outgoing
wastes, which play a major role in the campus's environmental footprint.
According to the EPA, the average college student produces 640 pounds
of solid waste each year, including 500 disposable cups and 320 pounds of
paper. That's a lot of trash!

Recycling Campus Waste

Just how do you start a permanent recycling program? The best way to reduce waste at your campus is to set up a meeting to talk with teachers, school administrators, and your school's facilities manager, expressing your interest in creating a recycling program at your school. If you try to start a program that depends solely on the students' work, it may fizzle out after your star students graduate.

Start with a waste audit: with the support of campus administration, collect, sort, and weigh the trash coming out of your classrooms, cafeteria, or other building(s) in one day. Do this on a few different days in a few different rooms or buildings and average the results. Multiply that by the number of days that campus is in session and you will see just how big an impact you could have if you launch a reduction campaign.

While you are collecting and sorting your trash, see what the most common items are and determine whether any of these could be recycled or composted instead of thrown away. Consider office paper, magazines and catalogs, newspaper, cardboard, plastic, glass, metals, food scraps, printer cartridges, batteries, and electronics. All of these can be recycled, reused, or composted. You may be able to find a group of students that can do a waste audit as part of a class project to see the volumes and types of waste generated on campus, costs of disposal, and recycling potential.

After you research the current campus waste situation, identify your specific program goals, like reducing solid waste by 25 percent in the first year. Similarly, research which companies or programs could handle the waste (on or off campus), and look to existing recycling projects in your own community as models. Decide what your campus will recycle. Where will you collect these items? What will you collect them in? Will you schedule pickups on campus or drop-offs at a recycling center in the community?

Start by calling any local recycling and composting companies (find leads at www.earth911.com). They can help you identify opportunities to get paid for the waste you recycle or the organic compost you produce. Be sure to mention this to your administration!

Understand your waste disposal budget: are costs centralized or handled by particular departments? Although the revenue from these savings sometimes covers full costs of program implementation, you may need to secure campus support to launch and maintain the program. Or see whether your city, county, or state has funding programs in place to support recycling or waste-reduction programs. Will the program be run by campus staff, student workers, or volunteers? Will you contract with a local recycling company to provide the service? Who will oversee the program?

When you're ready to launch, place bins in high-visibility areas like classrooms, dorms, dining services, computer labs, offices, and student and staff lounges. Make sure that it's just as easy for students and staff to recycle as it is to throw something away. A big educational push is essential, for both students and staff; prizes and competitions can get your peers on board from the start. Good signage on and around bins is also crucial.

You may decide to launch your campaign with a pilot program that focuses on just one section of campus to begin, or you could start by focusing on just one day. Choose a high-waste area, such as a cafeteria or copy room, or a time of year when a lot of waste is generated, such as a locker cleanout day or dorm move-out day, and be prepared with recycling containers and a transportation plan for hauling the waste to a recycling or donation facility.

Use Nontoxic Products

Not only do campuses consume (and throw away) tons of resources, but some of this consumption also involves toxic and potentially harmful products. You can help change both the volume of consumption and the types of products consumed on your campus, while also ensuring they are disposed of properly at the end of their life cycle.

Join the Teens Turning Green: Schools (www.teensturninggreenschools .com) campaign and replace toxic cleaning products, arts products, and other school materials. Start by taking an inventory of all the products used in your school in these four areas: classroom, food service, janitorial, and grounds. First set up a meeting with the staff who purchase the products and inform them about the goals of Teens Turning Green: Schools. Ask them to show you the products and explain how they are used around school. Write down the names and brands.

Base your project on one of the four areas of campus or one of the specific products. You may choose products that are most harmful, or try starting with the easiest switches. Investigate the products, and identify greener alternatives by searching the Teens Turning Green: Schools website or visiting green products retailers. Find at least three greener alternatives for each product you want to replace. Test the effectiveness of these substitutes, either with the campus staff or as a research project for school. Using your conclusions, choose the most effective and cost-effective greener alternative. You can find greener alternatives on campus for pesticides and herbicides, toxic dry erase markers, conventional cleaning supplies, and so much more.

Buy Eco-Friendly Products

Eco-friendly alternatives exist for other products too, such as paper. Hannah McHardy didn't want to see paper from old-growth trees in her computer labs and classrooms, so she ran a campaign to transition to greener papers.

SUCCESS STORY
THE OLD GROWTH PROJECT After Hannah McHardy

experienced an old-growth temperate rainforest in the Pacific Northwest, her life was never the same. Hannah moved from Arkansas to Seattle her senior year of high school. In her new home she fell deeply in love with the ancient forest ecosystems, and on discovering that fewer than 5 percent of ancient temperate rainforests remain in North America, she decided to take action to protect endangered forests.

When Hannah learned that western Washington's schools were largely funded through logging on millions of acres of state lands, she and her classmates formed the Eco-Justice committee at Nova High School. The committee educated themselves and their classmates on the ecological and intrinsic value of old-growth forests. Hannah organized teach-ins at her high school and organized for students to attend the Board of Natural Resources meetings pertaining to 1.4 million acres of forests slated to be logged for public school funding. The high school students held a banner reading, "Don't clear-cut old-growth forests for our education." Hannah appealed to the state Board of Natural Resources to spare the old-growth forests and institute sustainable timber harvest practices. She spoke about alternatives to the proposed clear-cut logging, the benefits of intact watersheds, and the value of old-growth forests to future generations.

Hannah and the Eco-Justice committee then founded The Old Growth Project at Nova High School, where she and her classmates persuaded their administration to switch from using old-growth forest fiber paper to 100-percent post-consumer-waste, chlorine-free paper.

"Realizing that I could make even a small difference in **PROTECTING THE PLACES THAT I LOVE LED ME TO CONTINUE EDUCATING MYSELF** on how to have a more sustainable relationship with the ecosystems that we rely on." **—HANNAH McHARDY**

© David Goldman

Like Hannah, you can get your campus to switch from traditional paper products to greener paper. Post-consumer-waste refers to paper that has already been used by a consumer and then sent back to recycle. That's better to use than pre-consumer-waste paper, which can include waste left over from manufacturing. Many paper companies bleach their paper using chlorine by-products, including dioxin, a known human carcinogen. Totally chlorine-free (TCF) papers are the preferable alternative.

Reducing paper waste is also key. Encourage students to "think before you print," set up automatic dual-sided printing on printers and copiers, disable print job "banner sheet" presets, and encourage the campus administration to go electronic for forms and documents whenever possible.

Once you've greened your facilities, what's next? Integrating environmental education into a school's curricula is just as important as greening the facility. In studies about teenagers' knowledge of environmental science worldwide, the United States ranks far below average, actually falling near the bottom in comparison to students in dozens of other industrialized countries. How can your fellow teens help save the planet if they don't understand how it works? You can change that by bringing sustainability education to your campus.

SUSTAINABILITY EDUCATION:
IN THE CLASSROOM AND OUTDOORS

The educational impact of the classroom can extend far beyond tests and report cards. The green economy is one of the fastest-growing sectors of the economy, focused on solving environmental challenges while offering economic benefits. Asking your teachers to provide you with hands-on sustainability education means you'll be well positioned to make a difference (or even a living) contributing to the critical work of solving the environmental challenges your generation is inheriting.

Environmental Education

Integrating sustainability education into your school involves convincing teachers to bring lessons into the classroom; take students outside; conduct hands-on, real-world learning activities; and perform civic or service projects focused on sustainability. Environmental education can be implemented in many ways. For example, if you are interested in topics such as food and farming, biology or botany, convince an administrator or teacher to support outdoor classrooms, with greenhouses, gardens, rainwater catchment systems, and more.

For assistance, look to the experts. National Environmental Education Week (www.eeweek.org) is a week-long prelude to Earth Day each April, promoting environmental literacy and stewardship among more than 3.5 million students using lessons and activities for K–12 classrooms. If your campus doesn't already have environmental programming, meet with the administration early in the year to see whether your campus can participate in the push during National Environmental Education Week.

In addition to infusing environmental education into your school's curricula, you can extend these lessons and use the information you have learned through community projects focused on issues in your area that are meaningful to you, such as environmental justice cases, invasive species removal, neighborhood gardens, or even a restoration project, as Evin McMullen did in Ohio.

SUCCESS STORY

SAVE OUR STREAM Evin McMullen grew up playing in rivers

and streams and gained firsthand knowledge about riverine wildlife habitat. As an activist, she worked countless hours on the restoration of the original coldwater habitat of the Chagrin River to save the Ohio brook trout, a threatened species. Knowing that community education was the key to success, Evin started Save Our Stream (SOS). SOS made presentations to local schools, worked with local officials to post educational signage in local parks, and held community service days involving K-12 students in habitat restoration projects. Evin wrote a book about brook trout for elementary school students, distributed it to local grade schools, and was publicized in numerous local and national publications. Her book, *Where Did They Go? A Community's Struggle to Preserve the Native Ohio Brook Trout*, was later published by the Ohio Department of Natural Resources and used in classrooms in Ohio, Florida, Washington, D.C., and Seattle to teach about the endangered species.

© Drew Altizer

"IF NO ONE PAID ATTENTION to these streams and conservation efforts were stopped, then some of these streams could be turned into culverts and **SPECIES BIODIVERSITY WOULD GO DOWN THE DRAIN."**
—EVIN MCMULLEN

Evin made a strong case for how involvement in stream conservation would amplify the scientific lessons from the classroom. Like her, you can choose an issue or area that affects your campus or community. Find a teacher or an administrator on campus who will champion your work, then partner with other campuses, organizations, or city groups to plan volunteer service projects. On the days of your events, be sure to document your progress to show your campus, your community, and other campuses. You can do this by inviting media, taking before and after pictures, and inventorying trash collected or invasive species removed.

Recreation: Get Outside Already!

One of the best things you can do to boost the green movement is to help get people connected to the outdoors. People protect what they love, and you can't love the planet unless you experience it firsthand. Plus, getting outside is a nice break from all that hard work indoors.

Getting outside is a major focus of sustainability education. With Americans now spending an average of 90 percent of their time indoors, the need to expose students to the outdoors has never been greater. Getting folks outdoors is easy if you form a club at your campus devoted to a particular outdoor activity: surfing, hiking, biking, walking, boot camp, even kite flying if you want. It doesn't matter what you do as long as you turn people on to nature in the process.

People are more likely to protect the places they love, so get them outside and show them around! Even if you begin by taking a hike with a group of friends, you are involving them in nature, and you will find that they will likely begin to care more about environmental issues.

Once you have an event planned, advertise it to your friends through word of mouth, email, Facebook, or any other method you can think of. After you get more people on board, perhaps after a few events, form an official club and talk to your teacher about how to be registered or recognized on your campus. An article in your campus paper, an address on the morning announcements, catchy flyers, and a little local press can also boost your efforts to raise funds, attract volunteers, and organize larger projects. For gear discounts and training from experts, see whether your club can get sponsored by a local outdoor organization or sporting goods store.

FOOD

More than thirty million youth—one-tenth of our country's population— eat at least one meal a day on campus. With almost 20 percent of global carbon emissions originating in one way or another from the food system, greening our campus food chain is a critical part of being environmentally responsible. To focus your group's efforts on the food system at your campus, there are a variety of strategies, like ensuring healthy, organic options in the cafeteria, planting a campus garden, composting, and kicking the bottled water habit.

Eat Real Food

What you eat directly affects your health and your ability to learn each day, and where and how it was produced, shipped, packaged, prepared, and consumed contributes directly to your campus's ecological footprint. It is important to have sustainable food and drink options on your campus. Hai Vo radically transformed his unhealthy eating habits when he went away to college, by shopping for and preparing fresh fruits and vegetables from the local farmers market. When he saw what a difference it made in his health and personal life, he decided to bring those benefits to his entire university campus.

SUCCESS STORY
THE REAL FOOD CHALLENGE

Hai Vo, a student at the University of California at Irvine (UCI), mobilized hundreds of students on his own campus and took on a leadership role nationally to mend a broken food system. After discovering that $4 billion was spent annually on food at universities, he cofounded the Real Food Challenge at UCI to convince his university to invest in "real" food—food that is ecologically sound, community-based, and fair to farmers and farmworkers—supporting the health of students, producers, local communities, and the environment. Hai co-organized events that engaged more than five hundred campus and community members in leadership development, dinners, an educational series, and online networks, all centered on sustainable food systems. With a fellow student, Hai researched the percentage of real food purchased in their college dining halls, and provided concrete recommendations and policies for their dining services. UCI used these recommendations to help determine a plan for doubling their real food purchases within the decade.

© Han Shan

"Working with the Real Food Challenge on campus **GAVE ME THE OPPORTUNITY TO WORK TOWARD SOCIAL CHANGE** in a collaborative, visionary environment." **—HAI VO**

Hai started locally on his own campus and later served on a statewide committee that helped the University of California develop a system-wide, institutional commitment to 20-percent real food procurement by the year 2020. His work served as a model for the Real Food Challenge (www.real foodchallenge.org) network nationally, working to bring 20 percent real food to hundreds of campuses across the nation by 2020. You can join this effort, which consists of more than three thousand students and allies at more than three hundred campuses.

Hai was an advocate for supporting local family farmers. But if you love to get your hands into the dirt, you can start a garden that feeds products right back into your own campus.

Plant a Campus Garden

Starting a garden on your campus is easier than you may think. Even if you don't have a large plot of soil or a team of master gardeners, you can start with a simple classroom window box or a raised bed on the corner of your parking lot. Begin by gathering a group of five or more students who are interested in starting a garden on your campus. Talk to your campus grounds staff about empty spaces where you could potentially start a small garden, then work with them and your campus administrators to gain approval to use the space. If you can't start a campus garden, look for potential sites or community garden spaces in your neighborhood.

To build a garden bed, get some scrap wood, a drill, and hardware like screws and corner brackets. Calculate your measurements and screw the pieces of wood together to make a square or rectangular box. Be sure to ask a relative, neighbor, or friend for help if you need assistance drawing your plans or cutting the wood. Purchase enough organic soil to fill your bed. Research online or at a local nursery about what plants grow well in your climate and during the time of year you are planning on planting them—in fact, it's even better to find experienced gardeners in the community who will mentor your team, at least for the first growing season. Plant the seeds, and make sure you've designed a schedule of committed volunteers to water, weed, and tend the plants each week. Don't forget about weekends and vacations! Most important, make sure your campus knows about what you are doing, and give other students and teachers a way to get involved. Be thinking about how to expand your garden, where to put more beds, and how to get community members involved.

Encourage your teachers to find ideas for integrating the garden into a variety of classes and curricula, from health and science to economics, art, and literature classes. The world's most pressing questions regarding health, culture, environment, education, and the global economy cannot be adequately addressed without considering the food we eat and how it is produced. Your garden can be an effective tool in teaching these and other green concepts.

Finally, have fun and chow down! Share your harvest with other students by handing out veggies or making delicious jams and salsas. You can donate extra produce to a local food pantry or sell these at local markets to raise money, too. Take it to the next level by trying to get some of your food in the dining hall sourced from local and organic options. Growing a garden is a fantastic way to build community, so try to get as many people involved as you can.

Compost

Composting is the eco-way to recycle natural materials like food scraps and plant matter by letting them biodegrade. Not only can it reduce your campus waste bill (less food in the garbage can), but it also provides nutrients to naturally fertilize campus gardens. A good compost bin or worm bin has materials like fruits, vegetables, eggshells, and coffee grounds (no meat, bones, or citrus), along with small yard waste and leaves, paper, or cardboard boxes and egg cartons, to help along the process. Contests and an educational push can help get the student body on board; monitor the amount of trash each class or dining hall creates after lunch, and assess changes over time with the new composting program. If your campus uses Styrofoam plate ware, switch to biodegradable (or reusable) dishes.

Think Outside the Bottle

Pop quiz: how much more does bottled water cost than tap water? Would you believe that bottled water costs up to *ten thousand* times more per gallon than tap water? Not only is bottled water pricey, but it is also typically held to less rigorous quality standards than tap water in the United States, and some brands simply bottle tap water and stick a label on it. Just making the plastic water bottles for current consumption levels requires an equivalent amount of oil that could run a hundred thousand cars for a whole year, and shipping these bottles around the globe uses even more fuel. If you're fed up with the bottled water habit, you can join the Think Outside the Bottle campaign (www.thinkoutsidethebottle.org), using any of a number of tactics to kick the habit: selling reusable water bottles, setting up purified water stations, and ending the use and sale of bottled water at public events and in the dining hall.

Using food as a lens to address environmental issues is smart, because people love food, and most of us think about it three times a day (at least!). Transportation is another issue that students and staff confront daily, traveling to and from campus. Greening the commuting options is a great way to drastically minimize your campus body's environmental footprint.

TRANSPORTATION

Every year, 394,000 buses travel upward of 4.25 billion miles hauling students to school. All those miles are producing a lot of greenhouse gases along the way, but this doesn't have to be the case! Start by getting more folks out of their cars. Set up a Walk to School month (www.walktoschool .org) and make sure your campus has plenty of bike racks for student and faculty use. Most of the work students can do is on their own campus, but if you'd like to advocate for better alternative transportation, you can join up with Safe Routes to Schools to push for better walking and bike routes in your community (www.saferoutesinfo.org).

For those who live beyond walking distance, research public transportation options, and examine the campus's bus policy so the wheels on the bus can go round and round in a much cleaner and healthier fashion. If you drive yourself to school, pick up some friends. You can also set up a bulletin board or website forum on ride-sharing for your campus to minimize the number of cars following each other into the parking lot. Many students rely on the campus bus system to get to class. Some possibilities: transform existing buses from diesel to biodiesel and ban idling of buses—which is not only polluting but also wasteful, at 0 miles per gallon!

Go Biodiesel

Instead of using petroleum-based diesel, biodiesel buses run on vegetable oils. Using biodiesel eliminates sulfur dioxide emissions and reduces carbon monoxide emissions by over 40 percent and soot emissions by 50 percent compared with petroleum diesel. Andrew Azman wanted to find a way to reuse cafeteria waste oil. Little did he know his class project would revamp the entire city's transportation system!

SUCCESS STORY
FRENCH-FRY FUEL Andrew Azman, twenty-one, wanted his

campus to kick its petroleum dependence. As an engineering student at the University of Colorado at Boulder, he learned during a campus talk that biodiesel could power diesel engines with no modification and could be derived from waste oils. Andrew started a class project with a handful of peers to make a homemade processor to create biodiesel from leftover cafeteria grease. This project grew into CU Biodiesel, the nation's first student group devoted to the cause. Their goal? To bring biodiesel use to campus.

Andrew reached out to professors, the environmental center on campus, and a local biodiesel cooperative to build support for the project and identify funds. They won a $1,000 grant from their school and asked community businesses for financial and in-kind support, receiving services from two local companies—a welding shop and a hardware shop. Their pilot project was to revamp a single bus, working collaboratively with CU Transportation Services—the organization that ran the entire CU-Boulder campus fleet. They secured permission from the housing and food service departments to use waste oil.

The pilot project was a fantastic success and led to the expansion of the project to all campus buses, and eventually buses across the city of Boulder! The student body voluntarily increased their student fees to ensure the use of biodiesel, supporting CU Biodiesel with more than $120,000. Andrew's class project to reuse cafeteria waste oil grew to include an ongoing region-wide education program, construction of biodiesel processors for refueling, and a commitment from the city of Boulder to begin fueling its entire city bus fleet with biodiesel. CU Biodiesel (now called CU

Biofuels) continues to work on education and outreach issues related to clean fuels.

"It's healthier for riders, drivers, and the planet to **USE BIODIESEL RATHER THAN PETROLEUM**-based diesel. As an added benefit, it smells like french fries!" — **ANDREW AZMAN**

© Andrew Azman

Andrew reached out to an enormous number of partners and supporters, on campus and in the community, to go biodiesel. You can, too! Start by having a diesel vehicle donated to your campus (check with bus companies, shuttle services, and transport fleets, or search online for old vehicles). Even better, convince your campus bus service to convert their entire existing fleet to biodiesel! Enlist the help of your campus's shop class, technology department, or handy friends and parents to chip in their mechanical skills. If you will be processing biodiesel on campus, your chemistry teacher may be willing to help set up the equipment and program necessary to brew biodiesel on campus. After collecting vegetable waste and oil from the cafeteria staff or local restaurants and running it through your lab, you will have a clean green fuel that is practically free.

If you're not able to switch the campus fleet to biodiesel, you can at least curb the petroleum-based exhaust from idling campus buses and private vehicles.

Ban Idling Buses

Bus exhaust contains harmful substances in the form of particle pollution and poses an unnecessary health risk for children, drivers, and the community at large. In addition to its contribution to asthma and other respiratory illness, the exhaust from petroleum diesel vehicles is officially listed by state and federal authorities as a cancer-causing agent. Compounded with health hazards, idling wastes fuel and adds carbon and pollutants to the atmosphere. In chapter 5, Politics, you read about Amir Nadav, who led a successful campaign to reduce Minnesota students' exposure to dangerous diesel exhaust, culminating in the passage of statewide legislation that banned excessive bus idling in front of campuses and directed facilities to relocate air-intake valves away from bus parking zones. Launch your own campaign with the advice and resources at www.earthday.net/noidling.

NEXT STOP: CHANGE THE WORLD

If you've read this book straight through from the beginning, you've already learned how to find your passion, create an action plan, recruit supporters, spread your message and educate the public, lobby politicians and pass legislation, use your consumer power, protest successfully, make media headlines, raise money for your cause, and, in this chapter, green your campus. All of this gives you a lot of skills to use for your future endeavors. Now it's time to think about how all of this new experience will help you position yourself, as an individual, for a future in the green movement.

RESOURCES

Alliance for Climate Education (ACE), www.acespace.org On ACE's site you can learn about the science behind climate change and get inspired to do something about it: learn how to start an action team, apply for funding, network with other students, and more.

American Civil Liberties Union (ACLU), www.aclu.org/standup The ACLU's youth site, Stand Up, contains lots of information about the right to organize, how to deal with campus administrators, legal precedents for campus organizing, and much more.

The Association for the Advancement of Sustainability in Higher Education (AASHE), www.aashe.org AASHE helps college students, administrators, and faculty throughout the United States and Canada bring environmental sustainability to colleges and universities. They give awards, host an annual conference, and provide workshops and publications.

Campus Activism, www.campusactivism.org This interactive website allows students to share activism resources, publicize events, and build networks specific to campus organizing.

Earth Day Network's Educators' Network, www.earthday.org/education Direct your teachers here for hundreds of lesson plans they can use in the classroom to teach you and your peers about the environment. They can also apply for grants here for your projects, share ideas, and more!

Earth Day Network's Green Your School Guide, www.earthday .org/greenyourschool This site has student action plans you can use to create strategies for projects from small to large, all over your campus. Their Student Activist Toolkit (www.earthday.net/actiontoolkit), written for students, by students, has specific step-by-step action guides and background information on many of the projects in this chapter.

Energy Action Coalition, www.energyactioncoalition.org The Energy Action Coalition leverages the power of young people to organize on college and high school campuses across Canada and the United States to win 100-percent clean energy policies at their campuses.

Green Schools Initiative, www.greenschools.net The Green Schools Initiative helps kids, teachers, parents, and policy makers improve the environmental health and ecological sustainability of schools in the United States. They offer tools like the Green Schools Buying Guide and calculators to determine paper and other resource use on campus.

National Environmental Education Foundation, www.neefusa.org Learn more about environmental and sustainability education and find resources for you and your teachers to use in and out of the classroom. Find themed lesson plans and information about Environmental Education Week as well.

11
CHANGE THE WORLD

DEFINE YOUR FUTURE IN THE GREEN MOVEMENT

Changing the world is hard work! You may know people who have suffered from activist burnout. But with a little bit of effort, it's possible to grow your skills and deepen your impact as an activist without losing your steam.

I've watched hundreds of environmental leaders get their start, and all of them seem to follow the same general approaches to keeping motivated, staying focused, and creating opportunities for growth. Consider the following methods if you want to craft a lasting career out of your activism work. It's really possible to turn your passion into your dream job.

GET INSPIRED

One of my best strategies for staying committed is seeking inspiration and new ideas from books, documentary films, and gatherings where I can hear success stories straight from the mouths of grassroots leaders.

Attend Green Events

College campuses host sustainability career fairs, teach-ins, lectures, and film screenings. Take advantage of these, even if you're not a student. Other annual events serve as hubs for the green movement to congregate, share stories, and get back to work, refreshed and renewed.

➤ Green Festivals (www.greenfestivals.org) held around the country spotlight environmental advocates and green living, including green consumer products and services. In fact, they're always looking for the next generation of green speakers: throw your hat in the ring to share your story with the crowd!

➤ Bioneers (www.bioneers.org) is one of the leading conferences in the country for environmental innovators of all stripes.

➤ The Clinton Global Initiative University (www.clintonglobal initiative.org) hosts an annual meeting for more than a thousand students, representatives of youth organizations, and university officials to discuss solutions to pressing global issues. They also offer amazing resources, funding, prizes, and coaching to develop action plans.

➤ Join college students, administrators, faculty, national nonprofit organizations, and many others at IMPACT: National Student Conference on Service, Advocacy & Social Action (www.impact conference.org) for one of the largest national gatherings of campus community members involved in service, activism, politics, and advocacy across philosophical and ideological lines.

➤ Organized by the students in the environmental law program at the University of Oregon, the Public Interest Environmental Law Con-ference (www.pielc.org) is one of the best conferences in the coun-try for environmental activists (not just environmental lawyers). With world-class speakers and a low price tag for students, it is no wonder David Brower never missed it for eighteen years in a row.

Read Great Books

Another way to stay inspired is to read thought-provoking books about green topics or initiate a reading circle within your activist group to discuss issues related to environmental change. It's possible to develop a much deeper understanding of an issue collectively through discussion than any one individual can generate alone. Use the books on this top-notch reading list as a starting point for generating conversation:

AGRICULTURE

Fast Food Nation: The Dark Side of the All-American Meal by Eric Schlosser. New York: Harper Perennial, 2005.

In Defense of Food: An Eater's Manifesto by Michael Pollan. New York: Penguin, 2009.

Stuffed and Starved: The Hidden Battle for the World Food System by Raj Patel. Hoboken, NJ: Melville House, 2008.

CLIMATE CHANGE AND GREEN ENERGY

An Inconvenient Truth: The Planetary Emergency of Global Warming and What We Can Do About It by Al Gore. New York: Rodale Books, 2006.

Climate Solutions: A Citizen's Guide by Peter Barnes. White River Junction, VT: Chelsea Green Publishing, 2008.

The End of Nature by Bill McKibben. New York: Random House, 2006.

Field Notes from a Catastrophe: Man, Nature, and Climate Change by Elizabeth Kolbert. New York: Bloomsbury USA, 2006.

ECONOMICS AND BUSINESS

The Bridge at the Edge of the World: Capitalism, the Environment, and Crossing from Crisis to Sustainability by Gus Speth. New Haven, CT: Yale University Press, 2009.

Common Wealth: Economics for a Crowded Planet by Jeffrey D. Sachs. New York: Penguin, 2009.

Confessions of a Radical Industrialist: Profits, People, Purpose—Doing Business by Respecting the Earth by Ray C. Anderson and Robin White. New York: St. Martin's Press, 2009.

Cradle to Cradle: Remaking the Way We Make Things by William McDonough and Michael Braungart. New York: North Point Press, 2002.

The Green Collar Economy: How One Solution Can Fix Our Two Biggest Problems by Van Jones. New York: HarperOne, 2009.

Hot, Flat, and Crowded: Why We Need a Green Revolution—and How It Can Renew America by Thomas L. Friedman. New York: Farrar, Straus and Giroux, 2008.

Natural Capitalism: Creating the Next Industrial Revolution by Paul Hawken, Amory Lovins, and L. Hunter Lovins. New York: Back Bay Books, 2000.

CONSERVATION AND NATURAL RESOURCES

Crimes Against Nature: How George W. Bush and His Corporate Pals Are Plundering the Country and Hijacking Our Democracy by Robert F. Kennedy, Jr. New York: Harper, 2005.

The Future of Life by Edward O. Wilson. New York: Vintage, 2003.

Limits to Growth: The 30-Year Update by Donella H. Meadows, Jorgen Randers, and Dennis L. Meadows. White River Junction, VT: Chelsea Green, 2004.

ENVIRONMENTAL AND NATURE WRITING

A Sand County Almanac by Aldo Leopold. London: Oxford University Press, 2001.

American Earth: Environmental Writing Since Thoreau edited by Bill McKibben. New York: Library of America, 2008.

Desert Solitaire: A Season in the Wilderness by Edward Abbey. Austin, TX: Touchstone, 1990.

The Dream of the Earth by Thomas Berry. San Francisco: Sierra Club Books, 2006.

My First Summer in the Sierra by John Muir. New York: Mariner Books, 1998.

Refuge: An Unnatural History of Family and Place by Terry Tempest Williams. Lincolnshire, IL: Vintage, 1992.

Silent Spring by Rachel Carson. New York: Mariner Books, 2002.

Walden by Henry David Thoreau. London: Oxford University Press, 1999.

ORGANIZING AND MOVEMENT BUILDING

The Activist's Handbook: A Primer by Randy Shaw. Berkeley, CA: University of California Press, 2001.

Blessed Unrest: How the Largest Movement in the World Came into Being and Why No One Saw It Coming by Paul Hawken. New York: Viking, 2007.

Building the Green Economy: Success Stories from the Grassroots by Kevin Danaher, Shannon Biggs, and Jason Mark. Sausalito, CA: Polipoint Press, 2007.

Girls Gone Green by Lynn Hirshfield. New York: Puffin, 2010.

Letters from Young Activists: Today's Rebels Speak Out by Dan Berger, Chesa Boudin, and Kenyon Farrow. New York: Nation Books, 2005.

One Makes the Difference by Julia Butterfly Hill. New York: HarperOne, 2002.

Organizing for Social Change: Midwest Academy Manual for Activists by Kim Bobo, Jackie Kendall, and Steve Max. Santa Ana, CA: The Forum Press, 2010.

Politics the Wellstone Way: How to Elect Progressive Candidates and Win on Issues by Wellstone Action. Minneapolis, MN: University of Minnesota Press, 2005.

Rules for Radicals by Saul D. Alinsky. Lincolnshire, IL: Vintage, 1989.

GREEN LIVING

Generation Green: The Ultimate Teen Guide to Living an Eco-Friendly Life by Linda Sivertsen and Tosh Sivertsen. New York: Simon Pulse, 2008.

The Lazy Environmentalist: Your Guide to Easy, Stylish, Green Living by Josh Dorfman. New York: Stewart, Tabori & Chang, 2007.

See a Movie

Watching a film is a quick way to understand the basics of a new environmental issue, and the power of strong audio and visuals can leave an indelible impact on the viewer. People often walk away from films with strong emotions—indignation, joy, sadness, hope—that can inspire them to take action on an issue. After watching the goose-bump-inducing Oscar-winning documentary *The Cove*, detailing the massacre of thousands of dolphins annually in Japan for meat, hundreds of thousands of people around the globe demanded an end to the slaughter.

For visual inspiration, search out documentary films from Ironweed Films (www.ironweedfilms.com), Green Planet Films (www.greenplanet films.org), or the Video Project (www.videoproject.com). Watch free short films online from Media That Matters (www.mediathatmattersfest.org) or the Oneness Project (www.globalonenessproject.org). The DC Environmental Film Festival (www.dcenvironmentalfilmfest.org) is the nation's largest green-themed film festival for youth; even if you can't attend, track down their films from your local video store or library.

Although you can get great ideas and inspiration from films, the best advice often comes from face-to-face conversations—and who better to converse with than friends in high places? It's time to find your mentors in the movement. But it's not just a one-way street. You've got lots to offer a mentor as well, like your youth, your vision, your creativity, your advice, and your networks.

GET MENTORS

When Alec Loorz of Kids vs. Global Warming started out on his journey of educating the public about the science of global warming, he made a list of his top three potential mentors: people that were the cream of the crop at educating the public about climate change. Of course, Al Gore of *An Inconvenient Truth* and The Climate Project topped his list, so he reached out to Gore's organization to ask for help. As you might remember, Alec was initially turned away by Gore, but ultimately ended up becoming trained by Gore's organization and has now shared the stage with Gore on multiple occasions. Now he's helping Gore take the message of stabilizing the climate to a new generation.

Dream big, and ask your absolute heroes whether they'll mentor you. You never know who might say yes. As you consider who you'd like to approach to be a mentor, start by deciding what help you most need. Support in fundraising for your campaign? Someone familiar with the media landscape? A successful small business owner who can help you launch your own green business? A lawyer to coach you through the process of turning your group into a legal nonprofit? The more specific you are about your needs, the more likely you are to find the perfect mentor.

Tell everyone you know about your efforts—give them your elevator pitch or send them an email with a short description of your work, and ask them for the help you need. If they can't offer help, ask them to give you the contact details for one or two people who might be interested in hearing about your project. The more folks you ask, the more help you're likely to get in return. And if people ask you for support in their own efforts, try your best to fulfill their request or direct them to someone who can. They just might repay the favor in the future.

Mentors are great for advice and guidance, but when you need to learn the basics of an issue or skill set, it's best to seek in-depth training and practice opportunities.

GET TRAINED

Why reinvent the wheel? Learn from the mistakes of others, rather than making them yourself. Keep getting trained—and encouraging your fellow activists to get training—to build a team that can tackle any obstacle that you encounter in your campaign. Training is available in campaign planning, fundraising, media relations, social networking, public speaking, and every other skill under the sun. Some of the best free and low-cost training organizations in existence are listed below.

> ➤ Campus Progress (www.campusprogress.org) offers trainings and conferences quarterly, plus grants of up to $1,000 and communications strategy support to student organizers working on advocacy campaigns.

> ➤ The Drum Major Institute for Public Policy's DMI Scholars program (www.drummajorinstitute.com/dmischolars) trains college students from diverse communities in the skills necessary to obtain and succeed in entry-level public policy positions. Scholars will learn to approach problems from a policy perspective and meet professionals doing this work for government, think tanks, campaigns, and advocacy organizations.

> ➤ The Greenpeace Organizing Term (www.greenpeace.org/usa) provides a semester of advanced training for student activists, incorporating international and domestic travel to assist with Greenpeace

field campaigns on forest protection, global warming, and other key issues.

- Rockwood's Art of Leadership program (www.rockwoodfund.org) is a four-day intensive helping social change leaders develop skills in communication, self-awareness, presentation, emotional intelligence, and team building.

- Ruckus Action Camps (www.ruckus.org) are intensive training programs focused on campaign development and nonviolent direct action skills. At Action Camp, participants split their time between theoretical workshops focusing on a wide array of organizing and campaign skills and hands-on technical training in nonviolent direct action tactics.

- Sierra Student Coalition (www.ssc.org), the student-run arm of the Sierra Club, has produced more than ten Brower Youth Award winners. With a presence on more than 250 campuses across the country, SSC provides great support, training, and resources, including fellowships for college and university students. Earth Island Institute founder David Brower was the primary architect of the Sierra Club's lobbying and political efforts as the club's first executive director from 1952 to 1969. Their Student Environmental Leadership Trainings, called Sprogs (www.ssc.org/sprog), led by the nation's top student organizers, are weeklong sessions geared toward high school and college students, in which participants learn to develop effective groups and tackle serious environmental issues using grassroots organizing and leadership skills.

- Young People For (YP4) offers year-long fellowships (www.young peoplefor.org) that begin with an all-expense-paid trip to a National Summit for Progressive Leaders, where fellows learn from other progressive leaders, attend skill-building workshops, and begin to refine strategies and tactics for running progressive campaigns in their home communities. YP4 provides advice, training, and an online community for continued support, and focuses on environmental and social justice issues.

➤ Youth for Environmental Sanity (YES!) Youth Leadership Jams
(www.youthjams.org) are weeklong gatherings of leaders ages
fifteen through thirty-five designed to foment collaboration and
creativity.

Many of these groups have networks that you can join once you finish
their training. You're never alone in your advocacy work—you are part of a
community of youth who are pushing for environmental solutions! When
you connect to a network of young environmental change agents, lots of
opportunities open up.

GET NETWORKED

By linking up with others, you're likely to be kept up-to-date on environmental campaigns, pending legislation, and movers and shakers, and you'll
be the first to hear of new opportunities within the movement. Free or low-
cost trainings are often offered through these networks, which are also great
opportunities to meet other cool activists. When you get stuck on a particularly tricky challenge in your own work, suddenly you have hundreds—or
thousands—of brains to pick for ideas and solutions. If you're not ready to
design your own action plan, or you like the idea of working on large-scale
environmental campaigns (too big for your local group to do alone), team
up with their existing campaigns and make change collectively.

Greenpeace, Young People For, and SSC are groups already mentioned
that have extensive networks, as well as the Energy Action Coalition,
SEAC, and the Student PIRGs mentioned in chapter 1, Find Your Passion,
and AASHE, mentioned in chapter 10, Green Your Campus. More amazing networks follow.

➤ Earth Force (www.earthforce.org) focuses on schools, teachers, and
kids ages ten through fourteen who want to create environmental
solutions in their communities. They provide curriculum resources
for teachers and opportunities for young people to be leaders in
environmental issues.

➤ National Wildlife Federation's Campus Ecology Program (www
.nwf.org/campusecology) works with students and faculty at more
than a hundred college campuses on a range of greening projects,

from transportation to environmental purchasing. They also offer
paid fellowships for student-driven projects.

- ➤ Planet Connect (www.planet-connect.org) is a social networking
  site where high school students can learn about current environmental issues, funding opportunities, green colleges, and environmental careers.

- ➤ WiserEarth (www.wiserearth.org) is a global online network for
  organizations and individuals working on all issues relating to the
  ecological and economically just restoration of the planet.

Many youth networks are youth-led and directed as well. Stepping into
a leadership role to run the network is great organizational development
skills training, not to mention a huge boost for your resume, making you a
competitive applicant for internships, jobs, and prizes down the road. And
as you'll see in the following section, being visible in the world of activism
can be a good thing for your career.

GET RECOGNIZED

Hundreds of thousands of dollars are given away every year as grants and
awards to activists under twenty-five—both groups and individuals. Are
you getting your share? Winning awards isn't about tooting your own horn.
It's about building your personal capacity for activism and bringing more
resources to your cause. Winning one award becomes the first domino that
makes winning other awards much easier. How? Well, winning a prize gives
you a great excuse to send out a press release. That media attention often
leads to (surprise) more prizes and support for your campaign, which leads
to more media, and . . . well, you get the idea.

Most awards offer a cash prize as part of the package. What if you had
an additional $2,500 to invest in your campaign—what would become
possible? Lots, right? On top of that, winning awards brings legitimacy to
your campaign and its leadership, particularly when you approach other
funders for support. So start applying!

- ➤ Action for Nature's Eco-Hero Awards (www.actionfornature.org/
  eco-hero) honor the work of eight- to sixteen-year-olds who have

been part of creative environmental projects. The annual award recipients receive a cash prize, certificate, and recognition at an awards ceremony.

➤ The Brower Youth Awards (www.broweryouthawards.org) honors six young people annually for their outstanding environmental advocacy. Each winner is awarded a cash prize, participates in an awards week and ceremony, and receives ongoing leadership development support.

➤ Do Something (www.dosomething.org) offers a slew of grants and awards on a regular basis, ranging from $500 to $100,000. The Do Something Award, their top prize, garners recognition on a televised awards show.

➤ The Gloria Barron Prize for Young Heroes (www.barronprize.org) honors dozens of outstanding young leaders ages eight through eighteen who have made a significant positive difference to people and the planet. The prize includes mentoring, leadership support, and a cash prize for higher education or a service project of the winner's choosing.

➤ SeaWorld/Busch Gardens Environmental Excellence Awards (www.seaworld.org/conservation-matters/eea) give a $10,000 prize for successful conservation projects to eight groups annually.

➤ YouthActionNet Award (www.youthactionnet.org) gives awards globally to advance youth-led social or environmental entrepreneur projects, and offers a leadership retreat and ongoing coaching.

TURN YOUR PASSION INTO A CAREER

Want to make your passions your dream job? You couldn't have picked a better time: green jobs make up one of the fastest-growing sectors of the economy, and there's a need for solar installers, campaigners, organic farmers, environmental bloggers, and green business owners (and the list goes on) like never before.

Landing a paid position is tricky without at least some volunteer experience and a strong network of contacts. When making hiring decisions, many environmental organizations and green businesses are judging candidates on their proven, demonstrated commitment to the environment, and one of the best ways to show that commitment is via your volunteer experience. On top of all of your leadership in your own organization and the networking you've been doing, consider adding to your skill set by landing an internship in the field. National nonprofits like the Sierra Club and Greenpeace USA are always looking for interns; you can also look into opportunities with your local green group.

A number of programs exist to train recent high school and college graduates in the art of organizing and help place organizers in permanent salaried positions.

If you're looking for a more structured internship and training program with peers from across the country, check out The Center for Progressive Leadership (CPL)'s New Leaders Program (www.cplnewleaders.org), which connects young people from underrepresented communities with paid opportunities in the progressive movement. In addition, CPL provides leadership training, coaching, networking, and community building.

Green Corps (www.greencorps.org) is "The Field School for Environmental Organizing," with a year-long campaign-based training program that consistently gives their graduates excellent skills in grassroots organizing and places them in jobs with top organizations. Training is top-flight and camaraderie is excellent as you work on organizing on several environmental campaigns for other organizations. The Student PIRGs (listed above) are also great stepping-stones to paid positions in the movement.

Once you're ready to search for a paying job, how do you find one? Idealist (www.idealist.org), the Green Jobs Network (www.greenjobs.net), Green Dream Jobs (www.sustainablebusiness.com/jobs), and Treehugger (jobs.treehugger.com) are great sites to find available jobs (and sometimes internships and volunteer opportunities). Want to work in higher education? AASHE (www.aashe.org) offers a job bulletin for sustainability positions in colleges and universities across the country.

If your ideal job doesn't exist, dream it into existence! Write up a job description for your model position, figure out why you're uniquely qualified to serve in that role, and then start brainstorming what company, university, or organization might be able to use your services. Set up an

TIPS FOR LANDING YOUR DREAM INTERNSHIP OR JOB

Know the organization. Before you make your first phone call or write an introductory email, do your research. It's a waste of your time—and theirs—to call fishing for information. That's what websites are for! Get familiar with their mission, the structure of their staff, their recent victories and current projects, the application process for staff positions, and the bio of any staff contact you approach. An hour of research in advance will show that you're informed and organized—making you stand out from the other cold calls and letters.

Know what you have to offer. You should be able to clearly articulate measurable value you've brought to your past organizations and jobs. Rather than using vague language, like "I educated the public about sustainable agriculture," try to put a number on it. Did you double your group's donor base, generate thirty media hits, or expand your grassroots group from five active members to fifty? Come prepared with two or three stories of your biggest successes, as well as what you've learned from your biggest failure.

Knock 'em out during the interview. The best way to ensure a great interview is to practice. Draft up all of the questions you imagine your interview might cover. *The 101 Toughest Interview Questions: And Answers That Win the Job!* (Ten Speed Press, 2009) is a great resource to help you prepare. Provide a friend (ideally a working professional) with a small list of questions and have her grill you; at the end of the interview, debrief with her and ask her which one or two things you could work on to most improve your performance. A few live mock interviews are more valuable than running over the interview in your head a dozen times.

Dress for the job you want, not the job you have. You want to be dressed at least as professionally as the folks interviewing you, if not more. When in doubt, dress up. You're more likely to impress your interviewer than to look out of place.

informational interview with your dream employer to discover more about their workplace, then pitch your position; or apply for an open position to get your foot in the door, and explain how your skill set might be appropriate for a position yet to be created. Particularly in the business world, you will need to make a compelling case for the financial value you can bring to their team. For example, your experience saving $40,000 through an energy audit and lighting retrofit on your college campus could be valuable to a big company looking for ways to create cost savings—even if they never thought to do so by going green.

Or try consulting—work on projects of your choice, have a say in how much you earn and your hours, mix up your offerings from workshops to coaching to on-site project management, and make a number of contacts in various venues—possibly leading to a sweet job offer down the line!

This list of resources is just a start—with the green sector of the economy growing so quickly, more opportunities are cropping up all the time. Many former Brower Youth Award winners were fortunate to craft careers out of their activist projects, so we know it can be done! Your passion and commitment to a cause is the biggest asset that will help you succeed in whatever you do.

➤ Jared Duval won in 2001 for protecting a local wetlands from a major construction project. He went on to head the Sierra Student Coalition, the national student chapter of the Sierra Club, and the largest student-run environmental organization in the United States. Drawing on his experiences, Jared was inspired to write the book *Next Generation Democracy: What the Open Source Revolution Means for Power, Politics, and Change* (Bloomsbury USA, 2010), in which he explored, among other things, the leadership styles of the rising millennial generation.

➤ Deland Chan won in 2001 for her work restoring a native species garden in New York City—promoting green space in urban areas. She went on to study urban planning and became a senior planner at the Chinatown Community Development Center in San Francisco, California.

➤ Jessian Choy won in 2002 for founding the Student Environmental Center at her university. Now, she can often be found on weekend nights researching toxic products to ban from her house. She completely understands that everyone can't be as obsessive-compulsive as she is about being green—that's why she has helped organizations create and enforce green policies for more than ten years. Jessian went on to work at San Francisco Department of the

Environment, where she developed contracts so twenty-eight thousand city staff could save money and comply with the city's cutting-edge green purchasing ordinance.

➤ Rachel Ackoff won in 2003 for her work running Fair Trade activist trainings for the Sierra Student Coalition, helping adult and youth activists educate the public about the threats that free trade deals pose to people and the environment, and to advocate for responsible trade policies. From that work, she positioned herself to join the Sierra Club as the Washington representative for their Trade and Labor Program.

➤ Max Harper won in 2003 for developing a sustainable living theme house and introducing organic foods to his college campus. He moved into the field of filmmaking and for four years created films focusing on the stories of the Brower Youth Award recipients. Using those skills, Max landed a job with the New Media Department for the Obama Campaign, piloting the "Blueprint for Change" videos.

Not all of these individuals made a career out of their original campaigns—but they all used those skills and connections to land their position (or create it out of thin air!).

YOUR FUTURE AND THE FATE OF THE PLANET

It's up to you and your generation. You can and will change the world. As you're reading this book, there are a billion teenagers on the planet. One billion! The youth environmental movement is getting stronger every day. Just think: if every U.S. high schooler turned down the thermostat by one degree, it would be like eliminating 100,000 tanker trucks of gasoline or taking more than a million cars off the road (source: Adam Werbach's fantastic speech, "You Were Born to Save the Planet," at the Teens Turning Green national summit).

Readers, you are now equipped with some of the best tools available for making real changes that matter. The advice and lessons shared here came from youth organizers just like you who collectively have hundreds of years of experience organizing in the green movement. All that's left is for you to use these tools to great effect.

Use this book. Take it with you to your planning meetings. Give it to friends and your younger siblings. Spread the word. Then share what you've done on our website (www.buildagreenmovement.org) so your story can inspire more activists.

We need people working on all aspects of the green movement. So choose your issue and start organizing. One of David Brower's favorite quotes was from Goethe: "Whatever you can do or dream you can, begin it. Boldness has genius, power, and magic in it."

INDEX